Renzo Piano
The Art of Making Buildings

Renzo Piano

The Art of Making Buildings

Royal
Academy
of Arts

Contents

President's Foreword
Christopher Le Brun

When Renzo Piano was elected an Honorary Royal Academician in 2007, the redevelopment of London Bridge was still in the planning. Eleven years later, the Shard has become as recognisable a part of London's skyline as St Paul's Cathedral or the London Eye.

Born in 1937 into a family of Genoese builders, Piano spent much of his childhood exploring construction sites in his native city. These formative years educated him in the art of making buildings. Three years after graduating from the Politecnico University in Milan, Piano had his first solo exhibition in London at the Centre for Advanced Study of Science in Art. Almost fifty years on, with a RIBA Gold Medal and a Pritzker Prize to his name, Renzo Piano returns to London to present the inaugural architecture exhibition in the Royal Academy's new Gabrielle Jungels-Winkler Galleries.

'Renzo Piano: The Art of Making Buildings' is the result of a close and trusting partnership between Kate Goodwin, the Academy's head curator of architecture, and Renzo Piano, Milly Rossato-Piano and their colleagues at the Renzo Piano Building Workshop and the Fondazione Renzo Piano in Genoa and Paris. We are indebted to Shunji Ishida, Giorgio Bianchi, Giulia Giglio, Stefania Canta, Chiara Casazza, Chiara Bennati and Elena Spadavecchia for their tireless support. The fruits of this partnership are visible in the breadth of material presented, and we are grateful to Renzo Piano's studio and our other lenders for their exceptional generosity.

Tim Marlow has supported this project at the Royal Academy. The exhibition would not have been possible without the commitment of Lucy Chiswell, Stephanie Bush and Nancy Cooper, and the talent of the graphic designers Atelier Dyakova. We are indebted to our sponsors: Rocco Forte Hotels, Turkishceramics, iGuzzini, the Italian Trade Agency, and Scott and Laura Malkin.

Finally, we owe our gratitude to RA Publications, who have created this fitting record of the work of a world-renowned architect whom we feel lucky to count among our membership.

An Architect of Dignity
Kate Goodwin

As you set out for Ithaka
hope the voyage is a long one,
full of adventure, full of discovery.
C. P. Cavafy, 'Ithaka'[1]

The first 1:1 prototype
for the IBM Travelling
Pavilion, Genoa, 1984

With a knowing smile that comes with age and a little twinkle in his eye that maintains his youth, Renzo Piano will say that architecture is an adventure and life a journey, 'full of discovery'. The expression reflects his zeal for living and for making architecture, and how closely he believes the two are tied. Architecture is after all a functional social art and the most durable way we can express human ambitions. With interests that range from the technical sciences to the arts, Piano is both a pragmatist and a dreamer. He talks about making 'a place for people' and in his buildings uses practical means to aspire to beauty and wonder, together with a civic purpose. For Piano, architecture is a process in which ideas are developed through a synthesis of research and physical testing, driven by imagination and curiosity. The key quality is an accumulation of skill gained through experience: 'artists are not those with a gift but those who master technique'.[2]

Piano – with his strong and loyal team – has developed an approach to the 'adventure' of architecture rather than a single style. He and his colleagues absorb the aspirations of a place and its inhabitants at a particular moment and combine a conceptual idea that meets human needs with a plan for how this might be brought into being, from structural systems to individual building components, working the design up, as Piano says, 'piece by piece'. They test ideas in scale models and full-size mock-ups of sections of buildings, in order to discover how a proposal – whether the whole composition or a technical detail – might look, feel and behave. Tellingly, Piano's practice of more than 150 architects, led by ten partners, that he set up in 1981 is called not an architectural office but the Renzo Piano Building Workshop.

Maker and dreamer

Renzo Piano was born in Pegli, then a small coastal town to the west of Genoa, in 1937. He was the son of a builder for whom building was a profession of the highest order and who gave his son a love of construction sites that is still very much present today. As anyone who has done so will know, visiting a building site is a visceral and exciting experience. The raw bones of the building are on display: nothing is hidden and elements absent from the architect's drawings are starkly present. This is where the combination of mass, scale and the performance of materials are tested and problems solved. The complexity of planning and the relationships between services and structure are clear, but it takes imagination to visualise what the spaces will become once they are populated.

When a young Renzo announced he wished to be an architect, his father was bemused: why would his son want only to dream of buildings when he could be the one physically to construct them?[3] But Piano had recognised the architect's potential to improve places and make a meaningful contribution to people's lives.

In resistance to what he saw as the self-serving intellectual rhetoric of the academy, Piano developed an interest in *making*, through relationships with mentors such as the Italian architect and designer Franco Albini, for whom he worked while studying at the Politecnico in Milan and immediately after; the French designer Jean Prouvé, who was to become a lifelong friend; and Z. S. Makowski, a British-based Polish engineer who was pioneering new developments in space-frames – lightweight structures constructed from interlocking elements composed in a geometric pattern, with sufficient strength to span large distances. Albini, for example, spent more than fifteen years refining his Luisa chair through five different iterations, experimenting with variations in materials, manufacturing techniques and how the components were assembled. This method of try and try again remains vital to Piano.[4]

Exploiting developments in materials and structural innovation to explore a new architectural language, Piano's early experimental projects possess a spirit of excitement that caught the attention of the likes of the young Richard Rogers and the renowned architectural critic and editor of *Architectural Design* Monica Pidgeon in the late 1960s.[5] Pidgeon put Renzo in a category of 'architects … [such as Mies van der Rohe and Pier Luigi Nervi] who found complete absorption in the manipulation and developments of pure structural systems in relation to human requirements for shelter, comfort and functionally useable space'.

Piano's exceptional ability to grasp the complexity of the technical aspects of building is evidenced through his strong working relationships and friendships with engineers. This was cemented early in his career, during the design and construction of the Centre Pompidou in Paris (pp. 36–39), where the multinational architecture team worked alongside the

Piano with his
associates Noriaki
Okabe and Shunji
Ishida in 1979

British engineering group Arup to realise their vision for an open, adaptable and democratic cultural building. Structural components and services were famously placed on the building's exterior, becoming part of the design aesthetic and leaving the spaces inside free for art. This project led to the establishment of a strong working relationship with the structural engineer Peter Rice, whose reputation as a designer was evident in his being only the second engineer to receive a RIBA Gold Medal for Architecture in 1992. Following the Pompidou project and the disbanding of the partnership with Rogers, Piano and Rice were in practice together from 1978 to 1981, working on experimental projects that included designs for a Fiat car, moveable housing and a UNESCO rehabilitation scheme. The latter offered a new model for community participation through a transportable cube structure that would open to create an information centre and community workshop space used to consider how to restore the historic fabric of Otranto in Italy. This formative creative and intellectual relationship continued until Rice's untimely death in 1992.

Unlike many other architects, Piano does not present his engineering team with an abstract form, expecting them to find a way to make it stand up. Instead, engineers are part of his process from the start, developing a structural strategy that is integral to the design thinking. The same applies to the services and systems that make a building work. As a result, Piano is often called a high-tech architect, although he does not employ technological innovation as a means in itself, instead pursuing technology wherever appropriate to achieve the desired impact.[6] This includes a sensation of lightness that makes resisting the force of gravity seem effortless. Even a stone building like the Padre Pio Pilgrimage Church at San Giovanni Rotondo (pp. 60–61) has a feeling of weightlessness, with its huge, anthropomorphic stone arches resembling bones that though heavy in weight evoke a sense of agility, of being light-footed. Equally important is creating a connection to nature that is ideological, visual and sensual, often replicating natural systems to achieve human comfort.

The Mediterranean Sea is a constant presence in Piano's life and psyche. He overlooks it from his house and studio in Vesima, just west of Genoa, and he has built yachts on which to explore it since the 1960s. He loves sailing and relishes the fine-tuning of form, structure and balance that enables him to optimise the way the vessel skims the water and is driven forward by the force of the wind. He says a boat takes two years to build and two to tune, the tuning achieved through knowledge gained from handling, feel and intuition rather than intellect. He applies a similar approach of refinement through testing to the design of his buildings. And the sensation of sailing – of lightness, of defying gravity, of a connection with the horizon and with the sky above – equally permeates his architecture. Evident in his first experiments with tensile structures, this has developed into a poetic sensibility that plays on what floating might conjure in the imagination and human spirit.

Indeed, for Piano, practical thinking is always balanced by an inclination for poetic dreaming. He uses metaphors liberally in his speech and draws them into his designs to crystallise ideas for himself it would seem and to paint a picture to help others to understand his ideas. He has referred to several of his buildings as a 'meteorite' or 'spaceship' landing

Piano sailing his yacht *Kirribilli* in May 2018

on earth, and drew analogies with the boulder in René Magritte's *The Glass Key* (1959), a painting he and his associate Shunji Ishida had first seen at the home of his client, the great collector Dominique de Menil. He often talks of the 'pachinko', referencing the Japanese arcade game as a way to imagine how he would like people to move through a building.

While for some this sort of imagining would amount to little more than fantasy, for Piano it is managed through systems that regulate how he works and perhaps even how he thinks. He splits his time between offices in Genoa, Paris and New York, in a repeating monthly schedule into which site visits and client meetings around the world are interspersed. Every project is tracked through a wad of sheets of A4 paper that contain marked-up drawings from the project's lead architect, sketches he has made on folded pieces of paper kept in his top pocket and (often indecipherable) notes in Italian, French or English, depending on office and client. Held together by a bulldog clip, each hangs on a hook on the office wall, with some 30-odd projects laid out in a grid pattern. (It is worth noting that the floorplans of many of the buildings designed by RPBW possess a strict grid that gives order to the spaces and defines circulation and services.) These stacks of papers move with Piano, between offices, his house in the mountains and even his yacht.

People and places
Because the act of building is to make a mark on a place that changes it forever, architecture needs to be not only of its time but also to anticipate the future. The best of RPBW's buildings achieve this with great success, thanks in part to Piano's ability to observe and understand not just a project's immediate surroundings but the wider social and economic conditions of the local context and to anticipate what a place and its people might want to be.

Piano has said 'an excess of tradition can paralyse you – so you need a balance between gratitude for the past and a desire for invention, curiosity for the unknown'.[7] Unsurprisingly, his buildings show awareness of and respect for history, but not veneration. This is well exemplified by his infill building for the Jérôme Seydoux Pathé Foundation (pp. 76–77) in the XIII arrondissement of Paris. Here the newly created organic form that occupies a tight courtyard typical of the nineteenth-century urban fabric seems fitting – yet entirely unexpected – because of its scale, materials and detailing. So successfully has Piano integrated a radically new form into these surroundings that his design seems almost to have been conceived by the building's original architects.

This layering of urban fabric is paramount in Piano's native Genoa. Bordered on one side by a steep mountain escarpment and on the other by an expanse of sea, the city has of necessity been built upon vertically over time, creating a dense environment full of hidden life. A large working port,

part Italian, part international – and the launching point of Columbus's great
voyage of discovery – it was described by Charles Dickens in *Pictures from
Italy* as 'abound[ing] in the strangest contrasts; things that are picturesque,
ugly, mean, magnificent, delightful, and offensive, break upon the view at
every turn'.[8] Walking through Genoa, Piano will point out the city's marvels
and idiosyncrasies, noting the layers of history and use, how old meets new,
and how the city mediates its relationship with the sea. Reimagining Genoa
has been a personal project for Piano, from the redevelopment of the Porto
Antico for the Columbus International Exposition in 1992 (pp. 46–47), with
subsequent upgrades, to ongoing discussions about the redevelopment
of the waterfront from Porta Siberia to Punta Vagno, including a new control
tower for maritime pilots.

    Piano's view of architecture as a vital contributor to civic society has
always led him to think beyond the immediate boundaries of site and brief.
His projects can transform isolated areas into vibrant urban hubs, as in the
case of the Parco della Musica Auditorium on the outskirts of Rome (pp.
56–59), where an outdoor amphitheatre creates a new communal space
and the buildings are laid out so as to generate a connection to a large
neighbouring park. This creation of public space both outside and inside
buildings is a theme that has its origins in Piano's initial competition design
with Richard Rogers for the Centre Pompidou. In a radical move for the time,
the team allocated a large portion of the site to a public piazza that
extended into the building's ground floor, challenging the elitism of culture
by removing it from its plinth and symbolically democratising it and making

it accessible. The gesture not only had an impact on how the building feels and functions, but created a new urban space.

The true success of a building, of course, should be measured not by the reactions of critics but by how it is used and becomes embedded in the identity of a place. Piano often says that the greatest compliment he can receive is when people tell him one of his buildings appears always to have been there. Acceptance is often not instant, however: his boldest buildings have sometimes taken a little time to be understood and appreciated. The Centre Pompidou is the clearest illustration of this, but it has also been the case for others, including the Shard in London (pp. 72–75). Piano likes to monitor the lived experience of his architecture and often revisits his buildings, like a parent checking on his grown-up children.

Although Piano has described architecture as 'a way of lifting enormous structures from the land to create a space for daily life',[9] his most powerful works have a sensitivity to human scale. A large building by Piano is often composed of smaller elements that have a relationship to the human body: the Centro Botín in Santander (pp. 88–91), for instance, is covered in ceramic discs that can fit into the palm of a hand and The New York Times Building (pp. 64–67) is covered in thousands of small-scale rods. There is a sense of the architect striving to respond to the individuals who inhabit these buildings, as well as considering how the structures interact with their urban context.

Gianni Berengo Gardin has taken photographs of Piano throughout his career; here, in Tuscany in 2007, on the day of the launch of *Kirribilli*

Piano considering
the design of the
Island, which brings
together models of
nearly 100 of RPBW's
buildings at 1:1000
scale, in November
2017

Responsibility and charm

Architecture is in many ways a service – both to a client and to society.
It is a complicated profession and Piano often likens it to an iceberg: what
lies beneath the surface is far greater than what we see above. Realising
a building is a complicated and drawn-out process, shaped by personal,
economic, political, institutional and governmental factors beyond
the architect's control. It involves numerous relationships that require
diplomacy, patience, persuasion, compromise and passion, to be managed
with tenacity and fortitude while maintaining a clear and shared idea of
what is to be achieved.

Most often a very good building – one that has vision, meets the needs
of its users and contributes to the greater public good – results from a
positive relationship between client, architect and consultants. Piano takes
his professional responsibilities seriously and his success is in part due
to his ability to manage and nurture such relationships. Undoubtedly a key
factor in this success is his distinctive charm, which seems almost
universally to seduce and convince. He greets everyone with outstretched
arms and a friendly smile, his posture denoting a relaxed self-confidence
and conveying a genuine interest in and energy for life. In client meetings
he listens carefully, while also displaying expertise, asserting authority and
exuding geniality. He paints pictures with words, turning practical
responses into poetry.

Widely respected by his peers for the quality of his architecture and
his professional conduct, he is a shrewd and pragmatic selector and editor,
knowing where to focus his energies on a project, with a client and in
running his office. He does not invent for the sake of it, instead often
revisiting and reusing ideas after adjusting them to new circumstances.
He sees the importance of being able to stand back and take an overview
of the project and to identify the aspects and details that he needs to get
involved in.

Piano often talks about the 'fil rouge' – the thread that runs through
his and the practice's work – as being an attitude and approach rather than
a style.

> Keep Ithaka always in your mind.
> Arriving there is what you are destined for.
> But do not hurry the journey at all.
> Better if it lasts for years,
> so you are old by the time you reach the island,
> wealthy with all you have gained on the way,
> not expecting Ithaka to make you rich.[10]

It could be argued that this 'fil rouge' is creating a more dignified world
through building.

A Conversation with Renzo Piano
John Tusa

I first met Renzo Piano fifteen years ago for a BBC Radio 3 interview. It was in his Paris office, near the Beaubourg, the revolutionary building which made his name and that of his partner, Richard Rogers. It was, he suggested, with all its pipes and tubes, a 'parody of high-tech', and not in any way a 'high-tech triumphalist building'. But, he insisted, it was much more than a gesture: it was a 'provocation', and a correct provocation at that. I snapped him afterwards, wearing a light blue pullover, with his recognisable beaky profile, his easy, open manner. I remember his remark that 'culture is about curiosity, not intimidation'.

It was good to meet Renzo close to his then 'signature' building. He worked in its shadow but has never been overshadowed by what it was, how it was seen or what it stood for. He has an office there still.

Yet to begin to know or even understand Renzo, it is essential to talk to him in his office outside Genoa. Office is hardly the word. A series of stepped terraces move gently down the cliff edge of the Ligurian coast. His home stands immediately above, he lives literally 'above the office'. And the view! His beloved, character-determining Mediterranean fills the foreground and stretches to the horizon, a full 180-degree panorama. On a grey, January day, the sea was neither gentle nor beguiling, rather warning that it should not be taken for granted. Imagine the intoxicating effect of a sun-drenched Mediterranean light flooding into the work areas of the Renzo Piano Building Workshop. Imagine working there.

Did I mention its place on a cliffside? Literally. For the faint-hearted or frail, Renzo has constructed a glass boxed funicular lift complete with canvas chairs to access the office. Some lift! Alongside run four hundred steps. These are not there just because of practicality. Climbing the steps is part of the experience of working at the studio. I arrived in the lift. My conversation with Renzo started with those four hundred steps.

21

Renzo Piano: Four hundred! The rule in the office is that everybody that can walk up and down without taking the elevator should. It's good, because it's approaching the office slowly – slowness is a very important thing, the change of speed is part of the ritual and when you reach the top, you are in a different world.

John Tusa: And does that different world allow you to daydream about your buildings and problems that you have to solve?

RP: I don't know if daydreaming is the right word, but I have a system of recording images in my mind... I think it's not different from what everybody does. I know musicians that record sound in their mind. I have a very good friend that plays piano, for example – Maurizio Pollini – I know that he plays piano everywhere, even on the aeroplane, with the mind! What I do – more modestly, I don't play piano unfortunately – but I have a good habit of recording in my mind the place, the geometry, the topography.

That's the reason why I always want to go to a place. In the next couple of weeks, I have to go to Greece because we have to design a new hospital in Thessaloniki and in Athens. If I don't see the place, I can't do anything. The important thing is that you are keeping the visual reference in your mind, so that it's like having a little hologram in your mind that you can recall. I guess it's like a computer, you call back that image. You know when you talk to my friends the neuroscientists at Columbia University – 'Mind, Brain and Behaviour' is the building we have just finished – they tell you, you have a visual memory, which is in the back of the brain somewhere.

JT: Did you always know that you had that capacity, or was it something that the neuroscientists told you?

RP: I noticed that I'd got that capacity, but it's not just my capacity, it's everybody's – you just need to train that capacity. This is one of the most important things, because one of the biggest mistakes you do as an architect (well, you do many mistakes...), but one of the most typical is to be wrong in the scale of the building.

JT: Do you mean *just too big*?

RP: Too big, too small, or wrong in context... but if you want to be right, you need to know the place and you need to record the place very clearly in your mind, so that every time you think of the building, even the detail, you can almost put back again that picture. It's actually not a two-dimensional picture, it's a three-dimensional picture, it's like a hologram.

JT: So it will always be a question of being in the place, seeing physically where you are, and then…

RP: And then going back to that place every time you think of a different detail of that building, even when you think about a little detail – joining or colour or material – it's very good to have in mind that specific location. This is the point about scale and context that I'm trying to make. It's not something you can solve by making drawings, or, even worse, by making nice drawings, because if you make nice drawings, you are trapped.

JT: You then think, 'What a beautiful drawing. I've made such a beautiful drawing'?

RP: You will be happy, but you should not be happy. And by the way, if you make a bad drawing then you're unhappy, but you should not be *that* unhappy, because maybe the project is good.

JT: What you said about feeling happy… Two artists – one painter, one musician – said to me, 'If I ever do something which I *like*, then the following day I have to get rid of it and start from the beginning.' Does that make sense to you?

RP: This is of course a bit absurd, but it's quite true that you may easily fall into a trap of self-insurance, to fall in love with something, and that's the reason why it's so dangerous to do renderings. Today you ask a computer… and they never tell the truth by the way, they always lie. That's the reason I don't make a drawing that tries to be nice, I always do drawings that are just there to remind you of something. I think architecture should never forget that the drawing is only one of the instruments, but other instruments are conversations with people, walking, dreaming, thinking about context and all that.

JT: Have you ever started a project where, as it were, you saw the result at the very beginning? And thought, 'This is what the building will look like', and three or four years later, that is what you produced. Does that ever happen?

RP: Yes and no. For example, if I think about the Kanak job in New Caledonia, it was almost inevitable. I went there, it was my honeymoon with Milly. I took the poor lady for honeymoon to a place to do work! I'm totally insane…

JT: And you're still married to her…?

RP: Still married! But anyway, we spent three days there, sitting on the bay making a little sketch, with the sea and the wind blowing 25 knots. When you spend three days on the peninsula, in the middle of a blue sky, blue sea, you must be stupid not to understand that you have to flirt with the wind, with the breeze. So you know in some ways it was clear what we had to do: to use wood for example, that was vital. It was clear right at the beginning that we had to play with the breeze, we had to play with the sound of the building, because you are there and you feel the sound, so fundamentally, emotionally speaking, the building was there at the beginning. But it's not true that you sketch something and – like a genius artist! – that's that. This is bullshit, I mean honestly. This is what you said before: if you do something and that's that, you should be worried, not to fall in love with that gesture. Every time I talk to young people, I say 'wait a second, be careful, don't fall in love too much and too fast with what you're doing', because otherwise you lose the capacity...

JT: ...to be self-critical?

RP: Yes, exactly. I think this is quite important.

JT: Let me try a slightly different approach for a moment. Because I was thinking about seeing you again, and I thought I must start with *who* is Renzo Piano?

RP: Ah, well that's very important, ok, let's try to tell you the truth. The truth is that I don't really feel like an architect in a sense. I mean, yes, I am an architect, it's not a lack of love and affection to this profession, but the way I came to this profession is by being a builder – honestly!

JT: Still?

RP: Yes, I am still a builder. At the beginning, it was absolutely clear. It was my interpretation of legacy from my family and I had to be somebody making buildings. Actually, as you know very well, my first four or five years' work was just making pieces, making buildings, making constructions.

JT: So that's why you still talk about the importance of making pieces and making them fit?

RP: Yes, this was kind of the beginning... that was the way I was severed from academy and rhetoric and formalism. I still owe this a lot, but of course it is a bit stupid to say that I am still just a builder, because of course then you learn so many other things. You understand that being an architect is more than that, it's being able to make buildings, it's also being able to understand people.

JT: You have to be a listener?

RP: Yes and this is something that no school teaches you. This is probably one of the most difficult things, because sometimes the people that have a lot to say don't really talk, or they talk very slowly. You need a little bit of passion and also a bit of humility, you have to understand people in the community.

JT: And to change your mind?

RP: Yes, it changes quite a lot. But wait a second, listening to people doesn't mean that you do what people tell you to do! It's not being obedient, but it's about understanding the complexity. So when you ask me 'who are you?', I'm fundamentally somebody that loves making buildings, but at the same time, I wonder all day about *why* you do that building, and that's one of the reasons why, when you go around the office, you find that we are doing public buildings – schools, hospitals, houses of justice, museums, concert halls and libraries. We love these, because it's even more important from the point of view of community, life and all that. It's part of this idea that architects change the world in some way.

JT: And so *what* is Renzo Piano, if that is a different question, which it may not be. I've asked who is Renzo Piano, but *what* is Renzo Piano?

RP: Maybe it's the third element of this story. There is another dimension in architecture, it is not building, not community, but it is... what? Can we call it poetry? Poetry is a bit too much, but it's about beauty.

JT: You're not frightened of beauty.

RP: I am! But in the same time as you are, everybody is, and we also understand, we *all* understand, that it is impossible to get beauty, it's like a bird of paradise, it's like looking for Atlantis. You know, beauty is death: *inarrivabile*. It is something you can never reach and this is something more difficult to talk about. It's easy for me to talk about construction, it's also quite easy to talk about community and the common good, it's not that easy to talk about this, the third element, but, still, it's there.

JT: So you say the third element is beauty, poetry, all those difficult things?

RP: It's the only thing, it is the untold, it's what you cannot talk about. Beauty is one of those words, like silence, that goes away in the very moment you pronounce the name. I know it's impossible, but in the same time, every time you do a job, no matter which one, it's still there. The beauty I'm talking about is not cosmetic, of course, it's the beauty of transparency, the beauty of lightness, the sense of *levitas*, flying. There is a beauty in the Mediterranean culture, you know. In Italy, *la bellezza* is not cosmetic, it's something else. In Greek, *kalos kagathos* is not just beautiful, it's also good. And this is typical of all the Mediterranean words, even in the African languages. In the African languages, the concept of beautiful is *never* separated from the concept of good. This is fundamental. Even in English! You say, 'beautiful mind', yes? 'Beautiful mind' is not just because it's beautiful, it's something you don't just apply to the external beauty, you also apply it to curiosity, science, discovery, tolerance, solidarity. Beauty is something that's immensely complex.

JT: Would you say it's the consequencé of doing so many things which are the right solution to the right problem? Because you've talked of being a builder, an architect, and then this middle ground that you probably shouldn't talk about. And if you do everything else right, then someone else might say, 'that is beautiful'.

RP: Exactly, you got the point. What I'm trying to say is, if you do something right in construction, a social right, it's missing a third dimension which is the one we're talking about. You are missing *pathos. Pathos* is a Greek word. *Pathos* is not just passion, it's a passion for something that is complex to define, the beauty of a civic attitude, the art of living together. And all those things come miraculously together in architecture sometimes. That's why I'm talking about Atlantis, because Atlantis is something that you look for that you will never find, but it is this moment where everything comes together, and in the life of an architect, if you get close to that moment, I think that's already a lot.

JT: What kind of, if I can use the word, leader are you? Because you have many people working, you might say, with you? Or working for you?

RP: *With* me, for sure.

JT: But you must have leadership qualities, though you might hate that phrase. Why is it that people work for you and work with you?

RP: I think I've always been like that. I finished my schooling in Milan in '64. I was working in the office of Franco Albini in Milan... Franco Albini was a great guy, fantastic man, very silent. In the day I was working, in the night I was occupying the university, that was

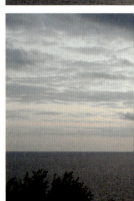

my job, a double life. And when you grow up in that atmosphere you know that the duty of the architect is, of course, to make buildings, but it is also to talk to people, to walk in the street, to understand. You grow up with this idea that creativity is something you share with other people. I've been working all my life like that, I don't remember one single moment when I was alone.

JT: But you are the leader. I come back to this, it's the Renzo Piano Building Workshop, so why should people and why *do* people work with you?

RP: I guess because the way we work is by everybody understanding that they are part of the creative process. I may have a special responsibility to take the decision finally, but everything comes out from a ping pong game. It's constant – I never sit apart, I never work alone, I never sit in my room somewhere – I don't have a room, I have a table! So I never sit down to do a drawing...

JT: You don't say 'that's done', then.

RP: I never do that, I always sit with somebody else. Then of course I put my fingers everywhere, but this is what I do! I think that is because fundamentally my office is not just my office: the decision I took twenty years ago was to give the property of the office to other people, so today I have ten partners and twenty-five associates.

JT: They actually physically, financially own a part of it?

RP: Absolutely, my share is 20%. This is also trying to say that I'm not the boss. I guess that everybody respects me because we've been growing together (maybe the youngest partner has been in the office for 25 years). We are not like that because we love each other, but because we grew up the same way. In the office, John, we don't really have to tell too much. It's almost like those mad people telling stories by saying numbers. You know, I say 'Five!' and everyone laughs, and that's enough.

JT: Ah yes, I've heard that joke before. But a building doesn't emerge from a committee, does it? What is a camel? It is a horse designed by a committee.

RP: I know, but this doesn't happen...

JT: So *why* doesn't it happen?

RP: Because we are not stupid and because I think we have a nice coherence, a nice integrity, in the office. I call this the *fil rouge*, what the French call the 'red line'. It is not a style... style is a simplified concept. It's more about coherence, about integrity, and I think that this exists in the office. It's also altogether about atmosphere. You know, when you live in a place like this, it's difficult to get wrong, because the entire system works in the right direction. Everybody is here, they come in the morning, we eat together, we share the office, so it's difficult to get wrong because it's almost like a good bakery where you make good bread every morning.

JT: You must have arguments though.

RP: Sometimes sometimes... we don't necessarily think in the same way, I think you can make a good thing by having different angles. It's very important to keep in mind that architecture is not something you do only with architects. You also do it with engineers, first – engineers are essential in this office. You never do a sketch just like that, you always know that that sketch corresponds to something visible, and the engineers are immediately a part, they are never in an obedient role, they always have a creative role.

JT: Do you have a good engineering instinct yourself?

RP: Yes I think so. You know, one of the jokes we used to do with Peter Rice was to guess the size of a structure: I would say 'that much', and Peter would say 'that much', and normally I was wrong by 10% and Peter was wrong by 5%. He was always better than me, of course. The other thing we used to do with Peter was to measure. For example, 'How wide is that TV?', 'How thick is this?' I have this tape measure. So with engineers – with a *good* engineer – you have to work that way and, myself, because I grew up in a builder family, and because my first four or five years were about making pieces, making tests, I experienced from that a kind of pleasure. When I think about a column, and you have a building on top of that column, I quite immediately think about the weight. How much is the weight, if you have four floors on that column? Something like 10,000 tons, maybe 9,000. I'm never wrong by 10 times, I'm wrong by 10%.

JT: Yes but that's an important margin, isn't it? Crucial!

RP: Yes, but still you understand the scale. This is something I do all the time myself, and we do this in the office – we do this game, still! Again, I'm going back to my hologram, you know.

JT: Renzo, I'm going to take you back because you mentioned that you were quite a bad boy in the 1960s. You were presumably quite angry with life, politics, architecture. What should a young Renzo today be angry about in architecture?

RP: I think the lack of roots in reality and construction. Computers are a very useful instrument, of course, because they add a lot in understanding and exploring options, but the bad thing about computers is that sometimes they make life too easy. It's like those pianos that play beautifully even if you play badly. I think that today young people should be rebels to the automatic idea that you push buttons to understand, because architecture is about being on ground - when you go on ground, you understand what you should understand, you know what you need, but also you discover things you never thought about. There's always a little genius of the place hidden somewhere - the *genius loci*, as the Latin used to call it - and if you go on ground, then you discover that, and if you don't find that, you find something else.

JT: Renzo, are you a starchitect?

RP: Eh?

JT: A starchitect.

RP: Ah, that's a terrible thing because it's coming up all the time. Well you know, no. No! I'm nothing like a star, I don't dress like a star, this is not my life. I don't spend my time at parties and all that, I don't make publicity. But also 'starchitect' immediately puts a little shame, a little shadow, on somebody, assuming that you act more for the form than for the substance. This is about superficiality and I hate that. This was what my mother kept telling me all the time. 'Don't play with this guy', not because it was bad, but because it's a superficial world for my mother. By saying you're a starchitect, it's almost like implying an accusation that you take more care about yourself than what you're doing. It is not a compliment. And also architecture, well I don't want to be moralist, but architecture is too important, it's actually a very important job. It's about creating a place for people by creating a better world, it's about bringing beauty, *that* beauty we talked about, to the world in which we live. That's fundamentally about giving people the opportunity to grow in a better place and that's the reason why that beauty is one of the systems to change the world, probably. It does it of course one person at a time...

JT: It's not a mass movement.

RP: But it is! One by one… because in the end it's about something creating better children, better people, better teenagers, you know, so it's a very important job. If you have that job, it's a bit like being a doctor, or being a politician, you must be bloody good. You must care about what you do, ethically. It's about ethics. If you introduce the 'star' stamp, you imply that this becomes more important than the rest.

Of course we enjoy the stature of somebody that people trust, but we don't make use of that, except when we feel we are right and when maybe somebody doesn't understand. Then sometimes I say, 'Look, why don't you trust me? We have experience. We know what we do.' But this is not because of the star syndrome, this is because of the experience, and also loyalty. If you are loyal for 50 years in a profession and not too bad, people should trust you, not because you are a star. But of course, you are treated with some reverence and some trust, you enjoy a special right to be trusted.

JT: How self-critical are you of your work?

RP: That's difficult, because I wish I could be more… being self-critical is probably the most difficult thing, you know very well, and the best way to be self-critical you know what it is? It's to get away from what you are doing for a little while. That's why for me travelling is not that bad. Tomorrow, for example, going back to Paris and finding the things after ten days distance is not bad. To be self-critical depends a lot on the ability you have to get away from what you are doing and to come back. This is something that, by the way, is typical of every profession. Even when you make a mosaic, you need to walk that close, because you work on a little piece like that. How much is that? Thirty centimetres? But then, afterwards, you need three metres. And I guess from time to time, I guess you also need also ten metres, because the mosaic will be seen from a distance. So you need from time to time to be up close, but if you stay there like that all the time, it's almost impossible to get self-critical.

It's also possible to be self-critical when something is discussed in the office, because sometimes there's an innocent voice saying – sometimes even the young people, the students – 'What about this and that?' Now, you have two different ways to react those things: one way is to say, 'No, no, no, forget it', the other way is to say, 'Hm, why not?' What you say is the most difficult thing because from one point of view you need to keep the direction, of course, because otherwise you go nowhere, but from another point of view you need to be able in the teamwork or by getting

away and getting closer again, you need to announce your ability to see things and to be critical.

JT: Finally perhaps, do you look back at your buildings and do a personal critique of your buildings over time? Do you look and say, 'Do you know, that one really worked, that one didn't.'

RP: Yes, I do it all the time. The truth is that the day that you're totally happy about what you've done, when you say, 'That's really perfect', then you should stop really. There's always something missing, this is what tortures you, in some way. It's not because you don't love - they're all children, they're all creations, so you love those creations - but at the same time, you understand that you've got to be better than what you've been. I mean I'm not talking about anything tragic because, thank God, we have never done something that wrong, but of course you always have something that you feel you should do or you should have done. The problem is that understanding what is right in architecture before it's done is not that easy. This is one of the tragedies. Architecture is one of the few cases where if you are wrong, you are wrong. If something is not exactly what you wanted, it's too late when you find out, and you feel guilty because what you've done is for everybody, for a million people.

JT: What do you hope that audiences, visitors, will take away from the exhibition? And what will they understand better about architecture, and about you, from this exhibition?

RP: I think probably this mix of the beauty, the poetry of construction, the art of making buildings. When pieces come together in the space, and then they hold, there is something there that's clever, well-crafted, but at the same time it's beautiful. I hope this will come out. And also that all this is not done for pleasure. It's done for making a better world, because it's about people, it's about creating a place for people, to stay together, to share values. Basically, making good buildings is a decent gesture of peace, it's about creating a place where peace is built. Peace is like a beautiful city: it's done stone by stone, piece by piece, one after the other, so I hope that people will go there and they will see those things and they will understand the funny pleasure of fighting against the force of gravity. It *is* a kind of pleasure, and the force of gravity, believe me, is the most stubborn law of nature.

Selected
Projects

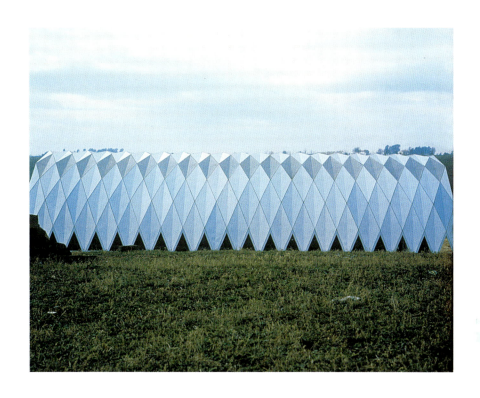

A selection of early works
Italy, 1964-71

Opposite: construction of a reinforced polyester pyramid structure, 1964-66

Above: the Mobile Structure for Sulphur Extraction, Pomezia, 1966

Left: the Italian Industry Pavilion at the Osaka Expo, 1970-71

The Menil Collection
Houston, 1982–86

IBM Travelling Pavilion
Rome (above) and York (opposite), 1983–86

Redevelopment of Genoa Old Harbour
Genoa, 1985–92

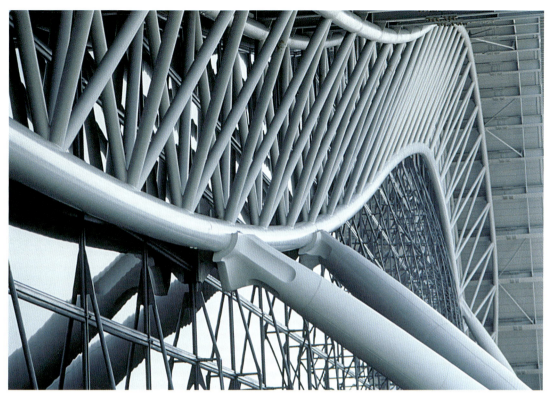

Kansai International Airport Terminal
Osaka, 1988–94

Parco della Musica Auditorium
Rome, 1994-2002

Padre Pio Pilgrimage Church
San Giovanni Rotondo, 1991-2004

Zentrum Paul Klee
Bern, 1999-2005

The New York Times Building
New York, 2003–07

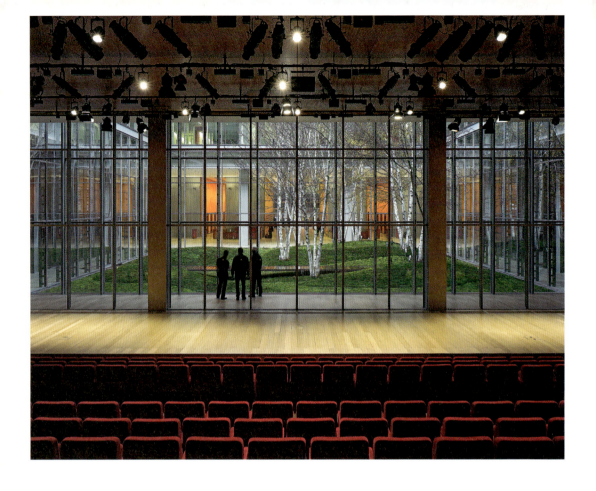

California Academy of Sciences
San Francisco, 2000–08

Central St Giles Court
London, 2002-10

Jérôme Seydoux
Pathé Foundation
Paris, 2006–14

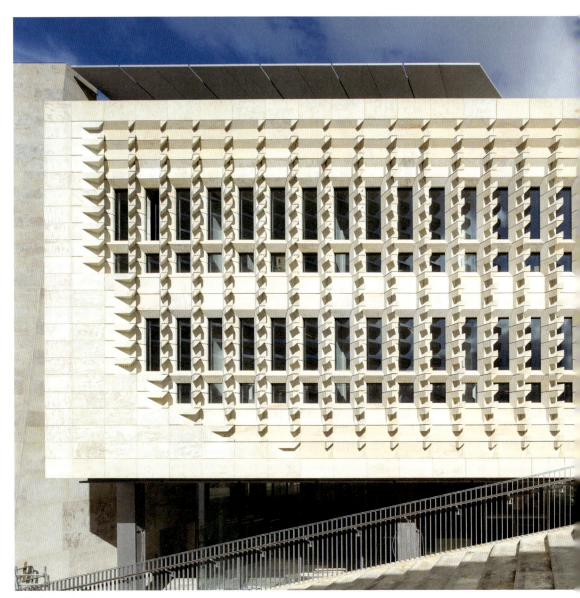

La Valletta City Gate
Valletta, 2009–15

Jerome L. Greene Science
Center (Mortimer B.
Zuckerman Mind Brain
Behavior Institute)
New York, 2007–16

The Whitney Museum of American Art at Gansevoort
New York, 2007–15

Stavros Niarchos Foundation Cultural Centre
Athens, 2008-16

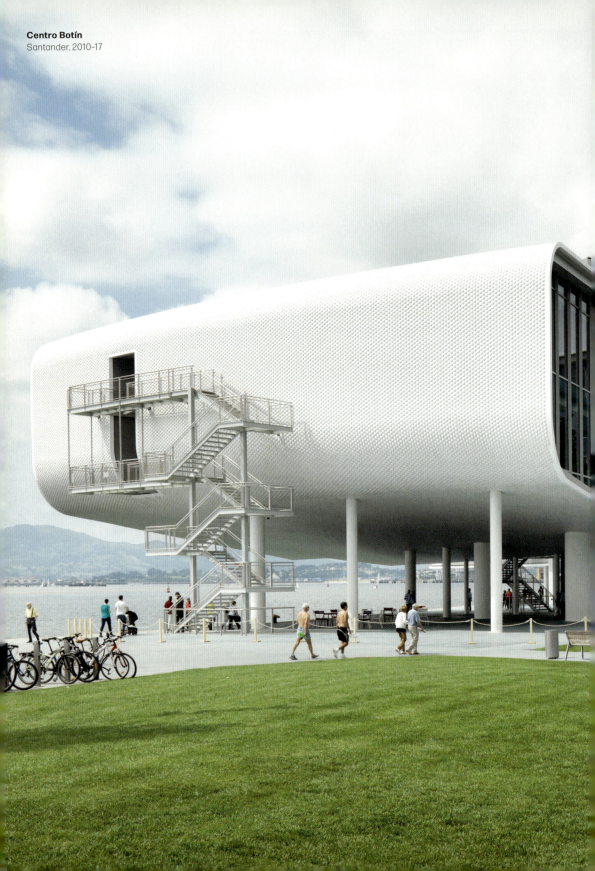

Academy Museum of Motion Pictures (in construction)
Los Angeles, 2012–present

Emergency Children's Surgery Centre (in construction)
Entebbe, 2013-present

Essays

A Renaissance Man
of Modern Architecture
Richard Rogers

Perched on a hillside above the Mediterranean, Renzo Piano's studio in Genoa reflects the warmth of his character, the range and joyfulness of his creativity, and his deep understanding of form, of lightweight structure and of light itself. With his sailing boat moored in the bay below revealing his alternative career as a boat designer, Punta Nave – Renzo's workshop and home – is the creation of a true poet of the built form, a renaissance man of modern architecture, and my closest friend for some 50 years.

Renzo and I met in 1968, when we were both at difficult moments in our careers. My first practice had run its course. With my wife Su, I had begun to explore new approaches to construction in the Zip-Up House, constructed from insulated panels joined with neoprene zips, and Parkside, the house we designed and built for my parents in Wimbledon. But we weren't breaking through or winning enough work to sustain our small office.

Renzo was working on his radical Italian Industry Pavilion for the 1970 Osaka Expo (p. 35), but had little work in Italy, where political turmoil and corruption made working as an architect very difficult. He arrived in London, where we were introduced by Owen Franklin, my doctor and the son-in-law of Naum Gabo (who Su and I stayed with when we were studying at Yale).

I was instantly drawn to Renzo, an elegant and animated figure dressed in 'English' tweeds that were much better cut than any London tailor could achieve. We soon started talking about cities, structures, buildings and their effect on society. Unburdened by having any work, we walked the streets of London, spotting opportunities for redevelopment, for improvement, for making the city more beautiful. The conversation we started 50 years ago is still continuing.

I visited his Genoese studio soon after we met, and from the first moment was bowled over by his work, by the beautiful models that he uses to develop ideas of form and rhythm in his buildings. His family construction firm had given Renzo a deep understanding and appreciation of technology and technique, and his love of sailing and marine engineering was visible

The two young architects on one of the Pompidou's external escalators at the time of its opening in 1977

in the lightweight cable-hung structures that filled his studio. His ability to think in three dimensions and to grasp holistically the processes of making has enabled him to bring the same lightness of touch and design intelligence to hospitals as well as houses, boats as well as cars, to planning affordable homes as well as building them.

Like their author, Renzo's designs are poetic, graceful, considered. As Renzo himself has remarked, Punta Nave and Parkside represent our shared desire to provide more than shelter; to express our 'aspiration to beauty, transparency and light as spiritual emotions'.

In the early 1970s Renzo moved into a flat near mine in Belsize Park, and he, Su and I decided to work together – three partners could be unemployed together as easily as two. Our first project was the ARAM Module, designed to be parachuted into trouble spots around the world, with a latticed steel core supporting modules that could be used as field hospitals, but also as schools, town halls, dormitories, or whatever else was needed. The ARAM Module, which could build itself with the central core forming a crane tower, was never actually constructed, but its open-structure and flexible function gave us a signpost to the future. Working with Renzo felt exciting, dynamic and fluid, our interests – in social purpose, lightweight structures and adaptability – suggesting a world full of potential.

That same year, Ted Happold from Arup approached us about a competition to design a new cultural centre on a run-down site in Paris. For several days, the four of us debated whether to enter or not: competitions could suck up a lot of time and energy to little effect and the idea of a 'cultural centre' felt rather staid, when decentralisation was the spirit of the age and the Parisian *evenéments* of 1968 were still fresh in the mind.

Our response to the brief, once we had agreed to submit an entry, was intensely political. We promised 'a place for all people, the young and the old, the poor and the rich, all creeds and nationalities, a cross between the vitality of Times Square and the cultural richness of the British Museum'.

The building would be open on all sides, with no single front door, and we gave half the site over to public space, which ran up the side on escalators and walkways. In debating and developing the design, Renzo and I provoked and pushed each other's ideas, as well as challenging the brief; as Renzo himself sometimes puts it, we were being the 'bad boys'.

The building itself would not be a single-purpose monument or temple to culture, but an open and flexible container, supported by steel cables around the perimeter. Each floor could be art gallery, library, university or play group. It was an open-minded concept, given form by Renzo's poetic sense of space and structure, order and proportion, and by the engineering brilliance of Peter Rice, who continued to work with Renzo and me for many years before his untimely death at the age of 57.

When the identity of our entry was revealed to the jury, nobody had heard of 'Piano and Rogers'; it was only our partnership with Arup that reassured them. The seven years we worked together in Paris was unbelievably intense, as the architectural and artistic establishment did everything they could to stop the Centre Pompidou being built. Renzo, who spoke slightly better French than me, became the diplomat, and the ringmaster of our growing team. Our friendship deepened in Paris; we lived together in the early months, we worked together through the night, we ate every meal together. Renzo insisted we never talk business at the table.

When the Centre Pompidou opened, it was pilloried by the press but loved by the public, with more visitors in its first year than the Louvre and the Eiffel Tower combined. Looking back, we were both more bruised than we realised. The partnership dissolved, but over time our friendship only strengthened.

Today Renzo and I speak at least once a week and see each other several times a year. Renzo and Milly stay with Ruthie and me in London, we stay with them in Paris, and we go sailing with them every summer. We talk about politics and policy, about family and work, about projects and practice. We are like brothers, incredibly close even when apart.

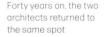

Forty years on, the two architects returned to the same spot

In Bottega
Fulvio Irace

The model-making
workshop or *bottega* in
Piano's office in Paris,
which opens onto the
Rue des Archives

Much has been written on the subject of architects' houses, very little on the other hand about their offices. Domestic space is considered to be an autobiographical declaration by the architect, whereas his or her office is mainly regarded as a project workshop, a neutral space subject to the demands of productivity. Yet nothing paints a more accurate portrait of the architect than his office. Work is carried out in the studio, of course, but clients are seen there too; the studio becomes the medium through which the architect shows his public face, his manifesto.

Rue des Archives in Paris cuts through the heart of the Marais from Rue de Rivoli to Rue de Bretagne, within walking distance of the Centre Pompidou (pp. 36–39), the impressive structure of 'Beaubourg'. Number 34, a restored *palazzo*, has housed the headquarters of Renzo Piano's French practice since 1991, when they moved from the nearby Rue Saint-Croix de la Bretonnerie, home of his first practice Piano & Rice Associates, established in 1977. The entrance to the office houses what is more often the room at the back: the model-making workshop, where projects are cut out and measured by hand. When you enter, the smell of wood and sawdust and the hiss of jigsaws cutting thin sheets of plywood provide the first clue that hands are not used here to click a mouse, but to model the embryos of future buildings.

Piano calls this workshop his *bottega*, as if he still lived in the Genoa of his youth when, after the Second World War, he used to follow his father around building sites.[1] From his father he learned the dignity of the trade and the need to get his hands dirty by handling materials. He has commented on a number of occasions that this is the only way 'genuinely to understand how a building is born, how a ship is built, how a chair or a table is manufactured'.[2] These long afternoons left him with lasting memories of the life of a building site, of trips round the docks, and of the marvel and fascination of cranes lifting heavy containers which hung suspended in the air, defying gravity. 'For me, the port was the sea at work, a fabulous world where even elephants might fly,' he has said. 'Ships coming and going, *bastimenti* [cargo ships] – *bâtiment* in French, which also means a building, a construction.'[3]

Since 1991 Piano's Italian office has been in Punta Nave, a few kilometres from the port of Genoa, between Voltri and Vesima, overhanging the sea. It is reached by a glass funicular, a metaphor for the way nature and engineering can coexist in harmony. The office hugs the slope of the hillside and looks like a greenhouse, another reference to the labour of the local farmers who, in this corner of Liguria, have created a landscape that bears the hallmark of mankind. Furthermore, the former farmhouse on the top of the hill has been skilfully but respectfully adapted to serve as the house of the architect when he comes to Genoa.

Whereas the Paris workshop forms part of the urban streetscape, the *bottega* in Italy is located at the lowest level, with only a flight of stairs separating it from Piano's office. The Punta Nave office has become an iconic space, often used by Piano as a background to portraits of himself. The workshop, separated by a glass wall, is its *sanctum sanctorum*, a busy working space, where there is also a display of historical souvenirs. At the back of the workshop, a long wooden wall has the appearance of a *tableau vivant*, with fragments of buildings and details of their construction –

Carlo Piano, Renzo Piano's father, on one of the family firm's building sites in 1960

buildings that have emerged from the Genoese studio – pinned to it. It functions as a museum of natural history, with fossils, minerals and skeletons of animals, extant or extinct.

This attention to the process of construction, to the improvised nature of the handmade rather than to the aesthetics of the result, to pragmatism rather than to ideology, reflects an approach to knowledge that chimes with the Anglo-Saxon culture of empiricism based on experience. It is a long way from the culture of idealism prevailing in Italy. This could explain the success of the Renzo Piano Building Workshop in America, for example, compared with the company's slow rise to popularity in Italy, its country of origin. The empirical approach, the basis of the scientific method, requires experimentation and constant verification. All preconceived ideas are rejected and the environment is assessed in a constant spirit of discovery and adaptation.

Some of the words in Renzo Piano's vocabulary have, over the years, become mantras. For instance, the word *bottega* to indicate the workshop where apprentices learn their *mestiere* (trade), or the expression *pezzo per pezzo* (piece by piece) to describe a way of making architecture that doesn't start from a set form to which engineering solutions must then adapt, but is rather born from the harsh confrontation with structures. Since his landmark 1982 exhibition in Rome of the same name, this motto has been repeatedly adopted by Piano as a trademark of his *bottega*.[4] Indeed, 'piece by piece' elevates the idea of continuous research, of the constant refinement of solutions that have previously been tried and, finally, of the close connection between architecture and design.

As Piano explains: 'the piece-by-piece method derives from man's instinctive propensity to manufacture and utilise every single component in the constructive process. There are more than 360,000 ceramic rods on The New York Times Building, for example (pp. 64–67): sometimes the individual piece is so small and is reproduced so many times that it becomes an organism – and yet it is still recognisable. This clever way of building avoids the obstacles posed by real scale in the environment.'

'Among these obstacles,' he adds, 'the most dangerous is the rightness of the scale. If you design a building then discover errors of scale when you are constructing it, it is impossible to rectify the errors. So, it is imperative to study the component parts first, pursuing your investigations in great depth. This is why the laboratory was born, where we make models – and even maquettes – to a scale of 1:1. The only two ways of avoiding errors are: investigate the component parts and build a mental hologram.'[5]

Piano's reference to 360,000 'pieces' of ceramic rods on the New York skyscraper calls to mind the legendary 50,000 small blocks of granite specified by the studio of Italian designer and architect Franco Albini for the Rinascente project in Rome. The English architectural critic Reyner Banham – who caustically reproached architects for their incapability to think of their

buildings as an organic unity of volume and structure – was to term the
building 'exemplary' for its integration of form, structure and installation.[6]
It was no accident that Albini's studio on Via XX Settembre in Milan was
the first significant stage in the young Piano's *Bildungsroman* – the first
stop on a journey of self-education in architecture in which the canons
of the traditional Grand Tour for trainee architects of the early twentieth
century were rewritten. Whereas Louis Kahn, Gunnar Asplund or Alvar Aalto,
for instance, took a classical tour following the traces of buildings, Piano's
tour resembled the travels made in the late Middle Ages by *clerici vagantes*,
who travelled all over Europe seeking the teaching they felt to be most
appropriate for them. Young mid-twentieth-century architects were reviving
this culture: Piano was not in the search of built examples, but of people
from whom to steal the secrets of the trade.

 Piano's *peregrinatio academica* was very unusual for an Italian
student in the 1960s, and it did not end when he gained his degree. In fact,
it lasted for most of the following decade, ending only in 1971 when he won
the competition for the Centre Pompidou. At last the chrysalis had
metamorphosed into a butterfly. During the vital years of travel, from his
graduation in March 1964 to winning the Beaubourg commission, a map
of Piano's travels reveals intense activity in which brief apprenticeships
(with Albini and Marco Zanuso principally) and teaching (between 1969
and 1971 at the Architectural Association in London) alternate. A number
of professional commissions followed, including contributions to the family
business in the Genoese district of Gli Erzelli and to the Italian Industrial
Pavilion at the Expo in Osaka, Japan, in 1970 (p. 35), plus frenetic journeys

between Milan, Genoa, Paris and London (with a single significant visit to Philadelphia in 1968). This gives some idea of the cultural nomadism that characterised the roaring years of the neo-avant-gardes and radical utopianism.

Piano's notion of a building as a machine in the first plans for the Beaubourg may have borrowed a few details from Cedric Price's *Fun Palace* (p. 113). With hindsight, however, these were marginal: Piano was always of the conviction that architecture that cannot be built remains simply design, or is utopian. The years of Piano's training coincided with an explosion of avant-garde ideas, from the experimental group Archigram in England to the Metabolists in Japan.[7] In fact, he himself was most attracted to the forms of utopia connected to plans for a 'lightweight' society being developed by architects such as Frei Otto, who at the time was pursuing the theme of the shelter and studying forms of pneumatic roofing.[8]

As he travelled the world, Piano's choice of teachers shows striking perspicacity and drive. Albini was undoubtedly the *Lieber Meister* who taught him the most, through his silences as much as through his scarce words. He taught him to deconstruct in order to learn how to construct, requiring him to dismantle and reassemble a Brionvega television in order to understand the logic of the industrial process. He showed him the importance of light as a regulator of space, which was to be a central feature of the museums designed by Piano from the Menil Collection in Houston (pp. 40–43) onwards. Finally, Albini conveyed the importance of manual skills and the physical nature of the object. After graduation,

Frei Otto's German Pavilion at the Montreal Expo in 1967

Piano met Marco Zanuso who taught him 'to work on the physical reality of things' and 'to get [his] hands inside production processes'.[9]

Piano's forays were never random – on the contrary, they endorsed his intuitive attraction to the comparison of practice, to be found in the teaching of building by the direct method. In 1965 he had a brief encounter in Paris with the French architect-engineer Jean Prouvé, later a member of the panel of judges for the Beaubourg competition. Already a veteran of Zanuso's lessons on lightweight prefabrication, Piano was instructed by Prouvé on the necessity of starting from the study of materials and manufacturing techniques; most importantly, Prouvé taught him that method in building is more important than form. As repeatedly reported by Piano himself, the French craftsman embodied for him the model of the builder. In his École des Arts et Métiers (not more than 200 metres from Piano's Parisian office) – not an academy but a school of life – he taught young people to work (but first to think) with their hands. 'I still remember one of his exercises,' Piano admits. 'He gave you a sheet of paper and told you to make a bridge that would join together two points that were beyond the extremes of the paper. Then he came back and rested his pencil on the top of your model bridge and if it collapsed, you had to start over again [...] So the search for form was linked to its static performance.'[10]

Later, Piano was to recall his list of forefathers: 'I learned from Zanuso, from Prouvé, from my father and from Albini to make scale models for every project. In this way, unconsciously, a project strategy is introduced into the building process that is typical of industrial design: you start with the physical attributes of a piece, then you develop the aesthetic, functional and volumetric implications.'[11] Between 1965 and 1966, when Piano was in London, he met Zygmunt Makowski, known for his work on reticular structures and the structural use of plastics and, for 22 years, Head of the Department of Civil Engineering at the University of Surrey, where he also was responsible for the creation of the Space Structures Research Centre in 1963.

Makowski soon introduced Piano into lively international circles, inviting him to participate in the first International Conference on Space Structures in 1966. At the conference he met Robert Le Ricolais,[12] who in turn invited him in 1969 to Philadelphia. This gave Piano an insight into live experiments with reticular structures and corrugated shells. He learned from Le Ricolais to look at nature's geometric configurations, and took part in experiments with triangular and hexagonal structures. He used these lessons in his own way in the reinforced polyester covering on his brother Ermanno's establishment in Gli Erzelli (1966-68). Again through Le Ricolais,[13] Piano met Louis Kahn, who was engaged at the time in the construction of the Olivetti building in Harrisburg, Pennsylvania. Piano was instructed to resolve the thorny problem of pyramidal skylights – a tribute

to the skill he had acquired through his collaboration with Zanuso on
the roofing of the Olivetti buildings in Scarmagno (1967) and Crema (1968).

The dogged energy with which Piano pursued experiment, his ability to
develop in his own innovative way, and the wealth of experience garnered
from his *maestri* led him increasingly to the conviction that architecture is
assembled, not modelled. His rapid passage across the international
chessboard contrasts with his slow, patient methods of enquiry, supported
by the model of industrial architecture he had developed that was
assembled 'piece by piece'.

It is not by chance that the two focal points of the Punta Nave office
express Piano's working philosophy. The first – more intimate and reserved
to practitioners in the atelier – is the model-making workshop, where ideas
are immediately confronted. The other is the *Wunderkammer* in the main
rooms of the foundation at the bottom of the hill. The astonishing sequence
of models (hung from the ceiling, arranged on a long table or even attached
to the walls) is the living manifesto of both his ideas: *pezzo per pezzo* and
learning by doing.

This portrait of Piano as an apprentice architect highlights his unusual
ability to keep a firm hold on the compass during a voyage that was
familiar to him solely through fundamental principles – otherwise it was like
navigating in the open sea. His pirate raids gave him an immense wealth
in knowledge: but they only could have been invested when safe at home.
As a modern Odysseus he has learned to hold himself in equilibrium
between a perpetual impulse to leave and an equal need to return home.

London, Fifty Years Ago
Lorenzo Ciccarelli

On 15 November 1967 a small exhibition opened at the Centre for Advanced
Study of Science in Art, London, which had been founded by the Italian
artist Marcello Salvadori a few years previously. On show was the work
of a young, unknown architect: 'Architectural Research by Renzo Piano'.[1]
Eighteen months later, in the summer of 1969, a second exhibition was held
in one of the most prestigious teaching institutions in the capital:
'Architecture Experiment: Renzo Piano at the Architectural Association
of London'.[2]

It is surely significant that the first two exhibitions of Renzo Piano's
work were not held in Italy – neither in Genoa, where he was born, nor in
Milan, where he trained – but in London, a city experiencing at the time an
extraordinary outburst of cultural and artistic effervescence. It was here
that the Italian architect chose to spend the years 1966 to 1971, years
that were to prove crucial to his artistic and professional development.
Why did Piano choose Swinging London? And for what reasons did
London, its architects and its critics extend such a warm welcome to
the unknown Italian?

During the 1950s and 1960s, public building projects and innovative
urban planning, promoted by successive Labour governments, were
studied with exceptional interest in Italy.[3] Low cost public housing projects,
the establishment of 'New Towns' and the widespread building of schools
and universities had a decisive influence on a generation of young,
socially aware Italian architects. Particularly engaged were those activists
in the Communist or Socialist parties who witnessed a reformist and
democratic building programme materialise on a grand scale in Britain.
Such programmes were having a hard time getting underway in Italy. Italian
architects and designers were not only attracted by the political and social
components of the British experiments, they also scrutinised with fervent
interest the technical and constructional aspects of British public building.
By using prefabrication techniques, British architects were experimenting

111

with industrialisation in a sector that had traditionally been the realm of the artisan.[4]

This would certainly not have escaped Piano's notice. He was hungry to find technical advances that would seamlessly and coherently combine with contemporary innovations of form. It was this inclination towards the most avant-garde techniques, a springboard towards a new beauty and functionality, that triggered the changes of direction that marked Piano's university career. In 1960, after two years at the Faculty of Architecture in Florence, an institution which had little appetite for technical innovation at the time, Piano transferred to the Politecnico in Milan. There, in the throbbing heart of contemporary Italian industrial development, he was able to pursue his growing interest in prefabrication and the application of industrial processes in the building trade. Following his graduation in 1964, having defended a dissertation on modular coordination, Piano immersed himself in audacious experiments with prefabricated structures made of plastics, moving between Genoa and Milan – cities that were then, with Turin, the major industrial centres of Italy. Between 1965 and 1968, with his customary inexhaustible curiosity, Piano embarked on a series of study visits to France, Britain and the United States. These adventurous trips gave him the opportunity to approach the innovators he most admired:

One of the exhibition panels shown at the Architectural Association in 1969

engineers and designers such as Jean Prouvé, Zygmunt Makowski and Robert Le Ricolais, unchallenged masters in the field of light prefabricated structures.

The British architectural environment, bubbling with vitality and with an eye firmly on the future, chimed with Piano's interests. London appealed to him with its relaxed cosmopolitan atmosphere and lively spirit of innovation – qualities not apparently offered to him by Genoa or Milan. The architect's heart and mind were captivated by the unrestrained inventiveness felt in the arts, cinema, theatre and fashion in mid-1960s London, where collages of the futurist cities designed by Archigram sparkled and the brilliant observations of the critic Reyner Banham were directed towards the use of technology in architecture. London provided a place where Piano's mind could feel at home.

And London certainly repaid his audacity. Following the exhibition of his work at the Architectural Association, Piano became a lecturer at that fearlessly forward-looking school, teaching there from 1969 to 1971.[5] At that time, the members of Archigram were also teaching there, along with Norman Foster, John Summerson, Charles Jencks, Reyner Banham and Cedric Price. Their input and support helped to confirm to the young Italian architect the appropriateness of his experimental approach. Piano's enduring friendship with Richard Rogers also began in London. Rogers, born in Florence and linked through his family and culture to Italian architecture, shared Piano's artistic and architectural ideals.[6]

Renzo Piano did not simply enjoy the cultural climate of London, he immersed himself in it totally. His personal vision of architecture, which was to emerge so forcefully in the building projects of subsequent decades, was nurtured during this time. In 1970, thanks to the editor

The Fun Palace, designed by Cedric Price for the theatre director Joan Littlewood in 1961

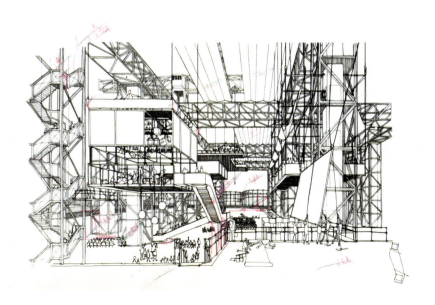

Monica Pidgeon, Piano introduced himself to the British public in a lengthy essay in *Architectural Design*.[7] In Piano's opinion, the goal of the most modern methods of construction was not to celebrate technique in any narcissistic way; on the contrary, it aimed to strengthen and revive the age-old links between buildings and cities – links that the uncontrolled explosion of European cities after the Second World War seemed to be in the process of destroying. Against the suburban sprawl that was beginning to afflict most cities, Renzo Piano contrasted the example of the Piazza del Campo in Siena, in which 'the city centre was conceived as a whole; multifunctional and yet integrated into a marvellously complex unity'. The iconic centrality of the Piazza del Campo is critical: it was to be the archetype of the parvis designed by Piano and Rogers a few years later in front of the Centre Pompidou (pp. 36–39). Although Beaubourg has been lauded for its engineered aesthetic and its modular construction, equally important are the symbolic and social connotations of the building, the unconditional embrace it offers to the city. We only need to consider the fact that almost all of the 681 proposals entered for the competition occupied the entire area available for the building. Only Piano's and Rogers's *machine joyeuse* left half the area empty, intending it to be a public piazza as shown in the plans.[8] A gentle slope encourages the visitor's steps and, as in the Sienese piazza, leads him or her towards the entrance of the cultural centre. Inside, the effect is prolonged in the spacious atrium, which occupies the ground floor of the building, like an interior piazza.

The aim of Renzo Piano's architecture is to create site-specific buildings that respect urban values. Piano's clear perception of the profession of architect, first fully expressed in the Centre Pompidou, evolved over the years through a huge variety of experiences and intellectual exercises, continuously refined in the celebrated buildings of the following decades: from the reconstruction of Potsdamer Platz in Berlin (pp. 54-55) to the Parco della Musica Auditorium in Rome (pp. 56-59), from the Manhattanville Campus of Columbia University in New York (pp. 80-81) to the cultural centre of the Stavros Niarchos Foundation in Athens (pp. 84-87).

The piazza is also at the heart of two buildings that have marked the return of Renzo Piano to London at the beginning of the new millennium, fifty years after his first stay in England. A well-designed 'public piazza' extends around the Shard (pp. 72-75) and invades the ground floor, connecting the splinter of glass to London Bridge station and the borough of Southwark. A piazza and courtyard are also at the centre of the Central St Giles Complex (pp. 70-71): five blocks, with bright façades made of prefabricated cladding in polychrome ceramic, stand in serried ranks around a welcoming central space. On one of the first sketches for the project, Renzo Piano scribbled 'the central piazza is the centre of gravity'. If these two London buildings testify on the one hand to the evolution of Piano's projects, on the other they show how his architecture continues to revolve around the same principles as his projects of the 1960s: 'piece by piece' construction, innovative use of materials, mastery of natural light and the urban value of the architectural project.

Sketch for the Central St Giles project, London, illustrating the pivotal role of the piazza, around which all the buildings of the complex revolve

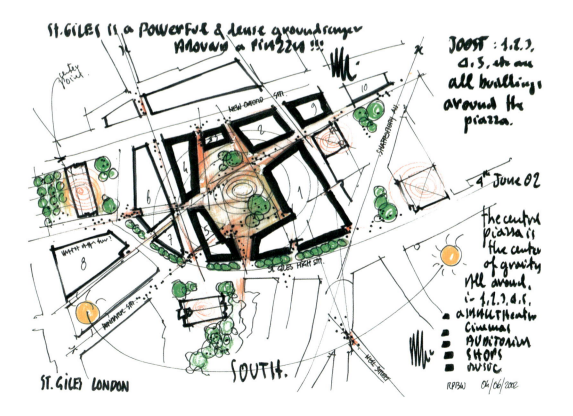

Floating Architecture
Susumu Shingu

It was 1989. I received a call from Italy at my small shack of a studio where I was working up in a mountain village outside of Osaka. The call was from the Renzo Piano Building Workshop in Genoa informing me that Renzo Piano had won the competition for the design of Kansai International Airport (pp. 48–49) and would be coming to Japan. He would like to see me as he had long been interested in my work. Thus it was that I met him in the Hilton Osaka lobby. He appeared carrying rolls of drawings in his arms. After a few simple greetings in English, I mentioned that I actually speak Italian. 'Mamma mia!' he exclaimed, not knowing that I had studied at the Accademia di Belle Arti di Roma and had lived in Rome for six years in the 1960s. At that moment any awkwardness in our first meeting disappeared. Besides, it turned out that we are the same age and we became immediate friends. His words then were: 'We've designed beautiful streams of air to flow through the departure lobby, but it's a pity they can't be seen. Can you somehow work out a way to make the moving air visible employing only a minimum of devices?' I had no reason to turn down such a tempting challenge.

To meet this challenge, I made many models, thinking in terms of 'fish that continuously swim in the air'. I even took my 1:100 scale model for the departure lobby sculpture to test it in the wind tunnel in Oxford. At this point, the man-made island for the airport hadn't yet been built. Whenever he came to Japan, Renzo was accompanied by Peter Rice. Peter always had a small triangular scale in his breast pocket and would go around measuring the models in my studio while Renzo and I focused on our discussion. Soon I became fast friends with Peter too – a quiet, thoughtful person. He was a man full of big dreams, working at solving many challenging and difficult questions in his field. At that time, Peter had a keen interest in the absolute strength of the joints in spider webs. It so happened I had just completed my picture book *Spider* depicting how a spider makes perfect webs. Peter and I promised we would study this amazing mystery together. I believe

Peter's great sense of wonder for the spatial art seen in spider webs – surely one of the finest miracles of nature – made it possible to realise structurally the 250-by-85-metre gigantic and elegant space of the departure lobby of Kansai International Airport without a single pillar. Seventeen 'fish' of around 15 metres in length made of yellow and blue sailcloth stretched on carbon fibre frames swim vividly and smoothly, carried on the air that circulates throughout the entire space. Sadly, though, Peter passed away in 1992 just before the completion of the airport. I wanted so much to further enjoy working on many more projects with Peter. I feel certain that the grief was even greater for Renzo. How we both miss him!

Since my first encounter with Renzo nearly thirty years ago, we have realised more than ten projects together. Among them are water sculptures such as Lingotto's *Locus of Rain* in Torino and Banca Italiana's *Water Flower* in Lodi. Others move by natural wind or with the flow of air indoors. Our first collaboration and biggest sculpture was *Columbus's Wind*, the monument for the Genoa Expo '92 to celebrate the 500th anniversary of Columbus's discovery of America (pp. 46–47). Various ideas were bandied about to try to show the image of the sailing boat *Santa Maria* before we reached the final form of nine 19-metre-high sculptures lined up along the wharf taking the shape of windmills made of triangular white sailcloth rotating in all directions. The ideas that surfaced and then disappeared in this process remain in my mind as valuable treasures. Making this monument was truly meaningful for me because the Port of Genoa was where I first stepped off the ship onto foreign land after a month-long sea voyage, dreaming at the age of twenty-three of becoming a great painter.

I often wonder how I have been able to continue working with Renzo for so long, with ever fresh energy for each project. What I admire about Renzo is that he makes it a point to consult me at a very early stage in a given project and explains to me the role he wants me to take in the context of the whole concept of the project. He does not want artwork that later gets attached to a building as decoration. Whatever the artwork, I think he is looking for the necessity of its being there. Since his ideas and what he asks of me are quite different for each project, it is always a thrilling adventure working with Renzo. That may be the foremost reason I have been able to work with him all these years. I have never worked with any other architect in this way.

The project for Maison Hermès in Ginza, Tokyo, arose out of discussions with Renzo, our client Jean-Louis Dumas, then president of Hermès, and myself. Jean-Louis's ideas about the best possible craftsmanship and his philosophy inspired me and from Renzo I learned about the balance of space in and around the building. It was so much fun for me to collaborate with such wonderfully talented people, getting new stimulation and coming up with ideas that I had never thought of before.

To be sure, my proposals are not always accepted as they are. Often they do not work out due to the wishes of the client, budget constraints and many other practical matters. Yet I fully enjoy every stage in the process of our work together. It is immeasurable how much I learn through each new project. I try to start from point zero to search for a new solution and, as a result, I come up with a work even I had never before imagined.

Piano and Susumu Shingu in May 1992. *Columbus's Wind* is visible in the background

Cosmos, 2016,
suspended in the
auditorium of the
Stavros Niarchos
Foundation Cultural
Centre, Athens

I continue to make sculptures that are, in effect, devices to translate into movement the natural elements that exist everywhere around us, such as air, gravity, light and water. Sculptures that are installed outdoors should have the necessary form, strength and mechanism to resist wind, rain and seasonal changes in the natural environment that can be quite severe; interior sculptures, on the other hand, should be highly sensitive to even the slightest wisps of air. These must be lightweight and equipped with smoothly rotating parts. Every gram and the minutest of dimensions greatly influence the balance and movement of the entire piece. This is the world of a mini-cosmos. I call such interior works super-lightweight sculptures.

So much unknown is still hidden in our planet Earth. The root of my work stems from keeping a fresh outlook filled with curiosity, as if I were newly born onto this planet, and when I discover something new, I show my surprise in shapes others can see. I want as many people as possible to know how happy I am to be born on Earth, our amazing planet full of abundantly alive plants and animals. That is why and how I have been, with childlike devotion, making machine-like contraptions of no practical use. Renzo sometimes calls me *pazzo ingegnere* (crazy engineer) which I definitely take as a compliment.

My most recent collaboration with Renzo is the Stavros Niarchos Foundation Cultural Centre in Athens (pp. 84–87), completed in the summer of 2016. I designed mobile sculptures for three locations: inside the auditorium of the National Opera, in its lobby, and in the lobby of the National Library. In the lobby of the auditorium, *Epic* welcomes and leads visitors to leave behind mundane matters and enter the artistic world of the theatre. *Cosmos* suspended from the ceiling of the auditorium gives the audience a way to feel relaxed with its soft movement and scattering of reflections; once the performance starts, it is raised nearly flush to the ceiling and disappears from the audience's view. And the third mobile, *Myth*, hung in the spacious library lobby whose walls are lined with countless collections of books, expresses the flow of time in silence. Especially in Athens, with its long history of art and culture, I cannot help but be deeply aware of the significance of the flow of time.

Ultimately, Renzo dreams of architecture that floats in space. That's what I believe. Whenever I fly out of Japan, I pass through the departure lobby of Kansai International Airport where I look up at the seventeen sculptures gently swimming in the air and I remember Renzo's words to me: 'Can you make the invisible air visible?'

Being a Client
Paul Winkler

The Menil Collection, Houston, showing the context of the 'village museum' within the neighbourhood

Dominique and John de Menil believed that art represented the highest aspirations of humankind. They often quoted their mentor Marie-Alain Couturier, the Dominican priest instrumental to the resurgence of sacred art in France in the mid-twentieth century, that 'a museum should be a place where we lose our head'. In her introduction to the book published in conjunction with the opening of the Menil Collection in 1987, Dominique went on to say 'Art is incantation. Like Jacob's ladder, it leads to higher realities, to timelessness, to paradise. It is the fusion of the tangible and the intangible...'[1]

Such strong convictions about the power of art and culture were instrumental in the development of ideas surrounding the de Menils' collection and its uses, including exhibition approaches and teaching programmes established at the University of St Thomas and the Institute for the Arts at Rice University, both in Houston, Texas. They would become essential in the search for a museum to house the collection permanently. In the end, the de Menils decided to build their own. In 1972 Louis Kahn was engaged to design a 'storage' museum on Menil Foundation properties, but the project was shelved after John de Menil's death in 1973 and Kahn's a year later.

When Dominique invited me in 1980 to return to Houston to help her realise the museum, her greatest concern was to find an architect who would listen to her ideas and give form, substance and beauty to her dreams. After looking at new museums in America and Europe for over a year, and at new buildings by architects suggested by family members and colleagues, she was frustrated, having seen bits and pieces that were of interest, but nothing that neared her vision. At that time Pontus Hultén, former director of the Centre Pompidou and a close friend and ally, said that she should meet Renzo Piano, adding that although he knew she wasn't a great fan of the Pompidou building, Renzo was a humanist and a very good listener.

We soon met Renzo over dinner at Dominique's apartment in Paris. After a lively discussion, we were convinced that he was someone with whom we could work. He listened intently and was intrigued with the basic concepts we presented for the museum, offering enthusiastic comments which assured his understanding of Dominique's dreams. We engaged him that evening, by letter agreement, to begin the journey to develop schematic and design drawings for a museum. A few days later Renzo joined Dominique and a colleague for a quick trip to Israel to look at a small museum in Ein Harod that Pontus had recommended for its natural light. Although neither found the use of light exceptional, it set the foundation of a strong working relationship between architect and client. The little museum became a laboratory for a few hours, where they observed together that the best light was from the north and determined that a zenithal source was preferred for illumination. Although there were no practical solutions offered at Ein Harod, much was gained by the visit. During the trip Dominique shared her dreams and ideas about the new museum. It confirmed that neither she nor Renzo were reserved in voicing their ideas, yet were respectful of the other's opinions. Renzo's sketches on the flight back to Paris reveal his first thoughts on a light-filtering platform roof.

A few weeks later Renzo and Shunji Ishida, the associate architect on the project, arrived for a first visit to Houston and the site for the museum.

Dominique de Menil's sketch of the second floor of the proposed Menil Collection

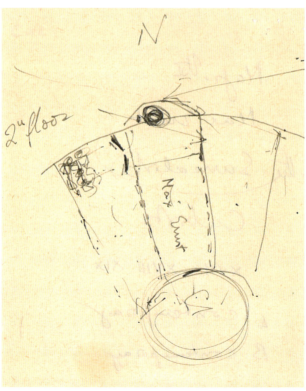

For five days they immersed themselves in the creations and activities of Dominique and John and their organisations: their home and collection offices at the house (designed and built in 1949 by Philip Johnson), the campus and buildings of the University of St Thomas (also designed, at the de Menils' urging, by Johnson in 1957), the Rothko Chapel (commissioned and sponsored by the de Menils), the Rice Museum and Media Centre at Rice University, and the Menil Foundation offices (a six-block property of vernacular wood-framed 1920s and 30s bungalows that was to be the site for the museum) and their neighbourhood. While Renzo may have expected a simple project to house a collection of art, he readily realised that this was a much greater adventure, one with patrons of broad cultural and humanitarian interests and an organisation that, although small in scale, was dynamic, exacting, progressive and passionate about its work, much like his own office in Genoa.

A very detailed building program specifying types and sizes of spaces desired for the museum's activities and the relationships among them, along with technical and security requirements, was provided, but the more important brief, the one which contained the conceptual ideas that defined the true nature of the project, was conveyed personally over long conversations at lunches and dinners with Dominique and a few of her colleagues. The exchanges between both parties helped refine the three basic ideas conceived by Dominique for the museum.

The first was that the museum was not to be monumental, neither in scale or size, nor as a commemoration to its founders. Renzo enjoyed the way Dominique conveyed this by saying 'I want a building that is small on the outside and large on the inside', which, he immediately understood, meant modest yet grand. It had to be incorporated into the environment of small residential buildings without overwhelming the neighbourhood. Renzo defined this as a 'village' museum, one which preserved a domestic neighbourhood and maintained and periodically added very special spaces for art. He understood the polemic of building a low horizontal structure, designed as a quiet space for contemplation and wonder, in a young city bustling with unfettered growth, trying to define itself and create a history, often by constructing tall towers that were icons to power and wealth.

He grasped the need to have the museum building focused solely on art and the direct activities associated with the collection, removing ancillary functions from the primary structure, including offices, a café, auditorium and energy plant, and placing them around the site in existing bungalows or new small buildings, thus reinforcing the 'village' concept. He integrated a relatively large structure of 100,000 square feet into the domestic environment by keeping the profile low, introducing a building with a module whose width reflected the width of the residential lots it faces, and by articulating the façade with numerous recesses and gardens. He further reinforced a connection with the vernacular by using a white-painted steel structure, with cypress wood cladding painted the same grey as the neighbourhood buildings.

Dominique's second notion for the museum concerned the collection itself. She firmly believed that only a limited number of works should be exhibited at any one time, all installed with great sensitivity. The remainder of the works should be easily accessible, in beautiful rooms providing secure environmental conditions. Renzo almost immediately conceived of what he calls the 'Treasure House' as the solution to this request. Originally envisaged as an underground space to maintain the low profile of the

The floor plan of the Menil Collection, showing the arrangement of the gallery and work spaces, March 1987

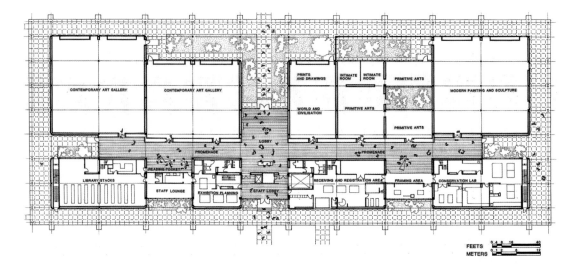

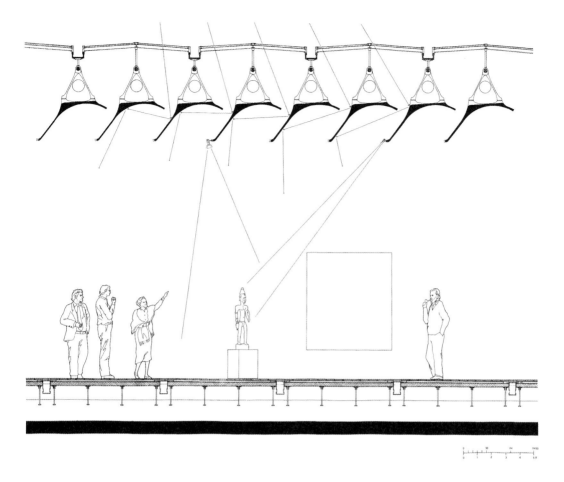

overall building, it was soon moved to form an upper level at the south
side of the building, to protect it from the dangers of flooding from
hurricanes, the primary natural disaster on the Texas gulf coast. This upper
level is devoted entirely to storage of art and research, with curatorial
offices centred between eight large storage rooms containing segments
of the collection. Each room is lightfast, secure and fire proof, with individual
controls for temperature and humidity levels. The paintings and framed
drawings are hung in a nineteenth-century salon style, from floor to ceiling
and frame to frame across the walls. Some objects are displayed on
pedestals, but most are highly visible in glass-fronted cabinets. Students,
artists and scholars have access to actual objects, which they may handle
and study intimately. Dominique's maxim that 'it is the real object that
puts you on the spot, that forces a reaction' has its testimony in the rooms
she conceived.

Related to her insistence that the collection be readily available, she
also desired that the essential functions of the museum, including a
research library, exhibition design studio, registration and records areas,
framing studio and conservation laboratories, be apparent to the visitor.

Piano and Rice
reviewing a 1:1 mock-up
of the leaf, April 1983

Renzo responded by creating a central circulation corridor through the length of the building, placing public galleries on its north side and professional spaces to the south. Visitors, who may glimpse into the latter work spaces from points along the corridor, as well as through large glazed openings from the exterior promenade around the building, are thus exposed to the daily life of the museum.

Dominique's third desire was to use natural light for illumination. Renzo was immediately intrigued and saw its potential in being the unifying factor in the project. Discussions of light can be far reaching and very subjective and our discussions on this subject were perhaps the most critical for the project. Renzo and Shunji had been joined at this time by Peter Rice and Tom Barker of Arup, who became the primary structural and services engineers for the project. Walter Hopps, who had been appointed director of the Menil Collection, joined Dominique and me. As a group, we finally determined that we favoured using natural light for the organic quality it brought to a space. Bringing light into the building would add a sense of the changing conditions of the day. Rather than a perfect and constant light for illumination of works of art, we would accept shadow and variations in brightness from room to room, and even wall to wall. This is the way one perceives light in a domestic setting, which adds a dynamic quality to both spaces and experiences.

Once this was determined, experimentation and research proceeded quickly. Theoretical ideas stimulated research on light conducted at Genoa.

Renzo developed the concept of a light-filtering platform roof as the unifying element for the building, creating scale models and then actual prototypes. Renzo used a 'leaf' as a metaphor and name for the primary component which would form the roof and lighting system, recognising the similarities between the two in filtering light, repelling water and in their integral structural ribs. The 'leaf' designed by Renzo and Peter was an invention and a challenge to realise and required detailed interaction between consultants and contractors. The complexity of the platform roof as built is belied by its simple and quiet, though predominant, presence. It was the perfect solution, addressing our concern that the platform not be too aggressive on the galleries, which would detract from the viewing of the artworks.

A group of talented and passionate people came together, shared their visions and convictions and fused their expertise and curiosity to create a highly technical and functional building, that yet was almost classical in appearance. Renzo achieved his ideal of designing a well-tuned piece that repeated two hundred times and made a building that was near perfection. Dominique inspired a building and formed a museum with the ambience where one could contemplate the wonders of art and lose one's head. And the world received, as noted by the late architectural historian Reyner Banham, 'a building that has put the magic back into Functionalism'.[2]

The key to our successful relationship with Renzo is that it was a symbiosis from the very beginning. Renzo's generosity of spirit, openness and curiosity were the basis for such an association. Five years later we came together again when the Menil Collection was presented the opportunity to add a pavilion in the neighbourhood for the permanent presentation of artworks by Cy Twombly. I was at first hesitant to ask Renzo to design it, as the project was very small by his usual standards and we already had agreed a preliminary floor plan with Cy to his own design, as well as his preferences for materials. Cy had asked me if I thought Renzo could 'put some light' into the building. Renzo's deep interest and intense investigations into natural light had begun with the Menil Collection and had continued to evolve ever since. This factor, along with the opportunity to revisit his concept of the 'village' museum by adding another structure into its fabric, intrigued him. Rather than seeing Cy's preconceptions as restraints, Renzo expanded and refined them to create what many consider one of the finest galleries for viewing works of art. He was joined in this adventure by his associate Mark Carroll at the Building Workshop and by Andy Sedgwick, engineer and natural lighting specialist at Arup.

The development of the exterior façade of the Twombly Gallery provides a perfect example of the symbiotic process in our working with Renzo. Cy felt that the exterior should be of sufficient mass to form a 'protection' for the more delicate works inside. Andy calculated the mass required to temper Houston's harsh climate in order to meet the stringent environmental conditions necessary in the galleries for conservation purposes. Renzo initially proposed stone as the material for the construction, but Cy believed it may appear pretentious in the neighbourhood. One evening Renzo and I were discussing the late buildings of Frank Lloyd Wright in Los Angeles, which had been made of concrete block. This stimulated the idea of using such a material for the façade. Renzo designed beautifully proportioned large concrete blocks made in Texas, with an integral colour of native sand and aggregate, which were placed on a single-stepped base to provide a strong yet quiet façade.

In contrast to the walls, the roof is an element of 'lightness'. It consists of suspended series of planes that constitute the ingenious zenithal lighting system. The interior light is almost palpable and, while providing perfect illumination for the paintings, it also imbues the galleries with a dynamic spatial quality that is transcendent. It is the essence of the building. As a final gesture before construction began, Renzo turned the Twombly Gallery 90 degrees clockwise to move the entrance from the streetside onto a green space that resonates with a small park to which it is diagonal. This move formed the potential for a new axis connecting an additional ten acres of Menil-owned property which currently is being opened to reinforce and expand the evolving 'village museum'. A new building to house the Menil Drawing Institute, designed by the Los Angeles-based firm Johnston Marklee, is currently under construction on the expanded campus and will open later this year.

Engineering Innovation
Alistair Guthrie

In the complex process of designing a building, the architect is usually the conductor of an orchestra of creative professionals who together provide the expertise needed to realise the design. These professionals will be experts in the design of the structure, the electrical power and communication systems, the safety systems, comfort control, plumbing, acoustics, lifts, lighting, energy systems, environmental control and a whole host more. The makeup of this team varies from project to project but there is a great benefit in established relationships within these teams, where shorthand communication can develop and ideas blossom from one project to the next. The idea of integrated design was very much the basis of Sir Ove Arup's vision when he founded the consultancy Arup in 1946. He was convinced that an integrated architecture and engineering team could best provide the total building design or 'total architecture' to which he aspired. The idea was that the integration of many parts would produce a better whole.

It was Arup engineer Ted Happold who initially encouraged the young Renzo Piano and Richard Rogers to submit to the competition for the Centre Pompidou (pp. 36–39). It was the start of Renzo's close collaboration with Arup which still lasts to this day. It is not just about two organisations working together, but how creative individuals in Arup are able to imagine together with Renzo and his team and then provide technical input to realise these dreams. Peter Rice, the eminent Arup structural engineer who worked closely with Renzo in these early years, and with whom he briefly had a practice (1978–81), explained this when he said, 'Engineers have a duty to humanise the construction process and so make architecture enjoyable again.'

I have had the privilege of working with Renzo and his colleagues in the Building Workshop for over 35 years. After studying Building Engineering, I joined Arup, working for Tom Barker, an influential Building Services Engineer who collaborated with Renzo on several projects, and Peter Rice.

My working career has been significantly influenced by my interactions with Renzo, working with him on many significant and groundbreaking projects. I have learnt to understand architectural ideas and devise engineering solutions to enhance them. My role has naturally changed over the years, and now is one of an overall engineering direction of projects, whereas when I started I was doing detailed calculations for others. From the first project until now I have provided technical advice on aspects of the design which influence the environment and how the building functions. This includes traditional engineering roles for the technical systems within a building but has in many cases extended to other areas such as day lighting, how the walls and roofs maintain a dry, warm or cool interior, and how the building responds to and influences the microclimate that surrounds it.

Renzo has always been keenly interested in the environmental aspects of the design and they have become increasingly important in a world in which energy consumption, climate change and wellbeing are dominant themes for responsible building design. In the early years there was an emphasis on structural design in Renzo's thinking. This was perhaps a result of his close friendship with Peter Rice and Peter's influence on the design. Renzo has always been keen to understand the technological aspects of the design, learning, absorbing and remembering in order to improve the next project. The goal of the design team is to strive for an integrated solution where all parts have a function but work together for a more complete whole. My first project with Renzo, the building to hold the Menil Collection in Houston, Texas, (pp. 40–43) was a demonstration of this and was very influential for me and architectural thought in general.

I remember an early workshop on the Menil Collection project held in Renzo's small studio built in the grounds of his family home just outside Genoa. At that point, there were just 10 people in the office, compared to the 150 across three offices in London, Paris and New York today. The purpose of the workshop was to find the solution for Renzo's idea of a single repetitive roof element that would achieve many of the necessary technical functions of the gallery spaces. These included a structure which spanned forty feet to create open flexible galleries, the exclusion of the strong Texas sun which would degrade the paintings, the filtering of natural daylight to provide quality display conditions, and the integration of necessary technical services: electric lighting, fire systems and air conditioning. We had prepared beforehand a matrix of these parameters to inform the discussions. Renzo's ability to grasp these and distil them into an integrated whole set the foundations for the project and led to the coining of the term 'leaves', which would together make up the platform roof. Renzo and Peter's experiments using structural materials in new ways led to the creation of these shaped light-control baffles, which block the direct sun and reflect daylight, from ferro cement and cast ductile iron, the former used predominantly in boat building. A critical point in the workshop was held in the garden, where Renzo sketched the form of the leaf on a large piece of paper laid out on the grass whilst the design team watched.

Collaboration in those early days between our offices in London and Genoa was challenging as communication was limited to telephone and telex. This made the sharing of drawings and sketches difficult and slow as we had to rely on post or courier. This was the root of the regular two- or three-day workshops where we came together in Genoa or Paris to work on the design. These have never been project organisation meetings that we often have with other architectural practices, but real, pen-in-hand design sessions. These are critical to all of the projects despite the increasing ease of remote information exchange. What always characterises these workshop sessions is the hours of preparation put in by the Building Workshop team, who make beautiful drawings which cover the walls accompanied by models, from large-scale representation of the site to a few crucial details made in the model shop. This enables Renzo to explain clearly the direction of the project, although he often needs to explain to clients that this is not the end solution, but rather thoughts along the way. It is sometimes hard to see a young intern watching Renzo marking with his famous green pen on a beautiful drawing that she has been up all night preparing.

The natural environment has always been a major source of inspiration for Renzo's projects. Often moments of inspiration came during the periodic workshops, orchestrated by Renzo where each of us, as collaborators, contribute ideas to the general discussion as well as providing our particular expertise. One such moment was the discussion surrounding the shape of the structures enclosing the Jean-Marie Tjibaou Cultural Centre in Nouméa (pp. 50–53). They were designed to face the ocean, allowing the cool sea breezes to be channelled into the building providing natural ventilation to keep the spaces fresh and cool. The client was unsure that this wind-driven comfort control would be sufficient in the climate, but with extensive hour-by-hour analysis of the weather and its interaction with the building we proved that it would be comfortable for 95% of the hottest month of the year, which alleviated their concerns.

A model of the Tjibaou
Centre is tested in a
wind tunnel

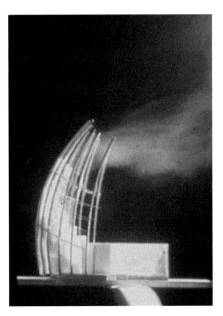

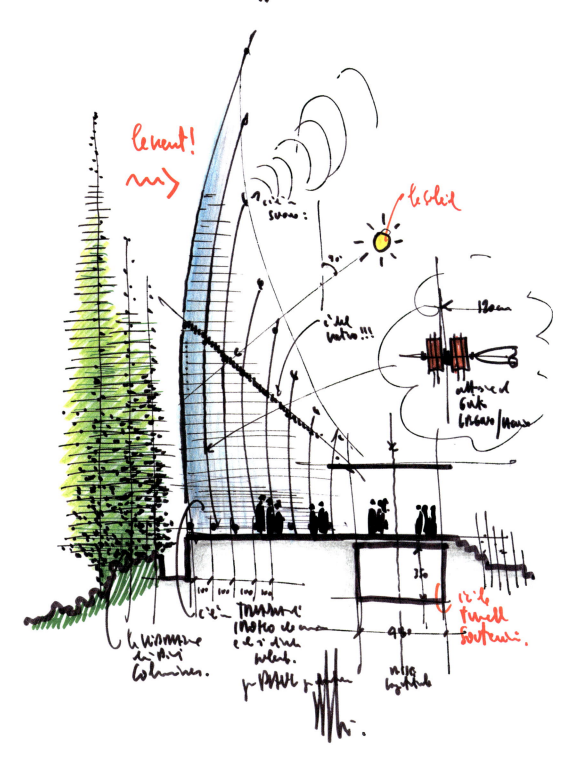

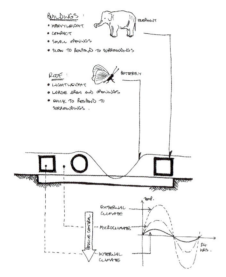

The Roof

Functions of the roof:
- Solar control
- Daylight and glare contro
- Variable thermal envelope
- "Elephants and Butterflies"

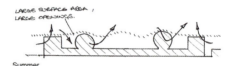

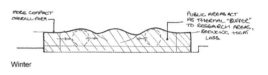

Summer

Winter

Sketch for the
California Academy
of Sciences, San
Francisco

The genius of the design was that the invisible wind was made audible as it passed through the open lattice at the top of the wooden structure so that it became apparent how the building interacted with it.

Another moment was in an early workshop for the rebuilding of the California Academy of Sciences (pp. 68–69). This building, located in Golden Gate Park in San Francisco, houses an important collection of natural history specimens. The director's vision for the building was to demonstrate the natural environment, use materials responsibly and minimise energy use. To support this, Renzo's initial concept was a planted roof, as though the park had been lifted onto the building. I suggested that if we made holes in the roof at the top of the domes which connected to the exhibition hall beneath, when cool winds from the Pacific Ocean blew across the park it would suck air through the building providing low-energy ventilation and cooling.

In many of Renzo's projects such early ideas – identified on a seminal drawing as points 1, 6, 10 or 11 – remain in the completed project. This is testament to strong collaborative early thinking, which is a hallmark of Renzo and his studio. Renzo's presence in these workshops provides not only charismatic leadership but also enables the group to grasp technical and aesthetic issues quickly. Sometimes this means the whole design team heads in a certain direction until Renzo announces that he has 'seen the Madonna', and the direction of the project is changed to accommodate an unexplained but often brilliant intuition. The summer holidays, which Renzo and his family spend on his boat, can also lead to change. If it's windy Renzo is occupied sailing but if the weather is calm his time is spent thinking and designing which leads to frequent communications with the office, sometimes resulting in a change of direction for the project.

The workshop method of working, although not unique, sets Renzo's studio apart from many other practices. Not all the ideas generated in these working sessions survive into the project. One of the initial ideas for the Shard (pp. 72–75) was to use the excess heat from the offices to heat the hotel and apartments at the top of the building. Anything left would be rejected through a visible wind-driven radiator at the very top of the tower. As the design progressed and detailed calculations were done it transpired – much to Renzo's and the team's disappointment – that this system used more energy than a traditional cooling tower solution. In this case, intuition was overruled by analysis. The Shard was also an example of an often-encountered conflict between, on the one hand, transparency and daylight through the façade and, on the other, the need for sun protection and thermal insulation. We used the approach developed on previous projects: multiple layers of glass and controllable blinds which are used on the different faces of the building as the sun moves round. This retains the sensational view, provides daylight and enables comfortable conditions with minimum energy used.

The solar collector roof of the Stavros Niarchos Foundation Cultural Centre in Athens (pp. 84–87) arose out of the challenge set between myself and the client at the first workshop to make this building energy neutral in operation. A large square was drawn on the site plan to represent the estimated area needed for the solar panels required to power the building. Renzo enthusiastically embraced this. The solar panels' shading canopy became integrated into the design of the building, although it was not quite as big as the original square, as we would have needed at least 40% more area to cover the building's energy needs entirely and this would have over-dominated its appearance.

I have always found Renzo's experimental approach to architecture, and his desire to push architectural and engineering boundaries with unique and better solutions, both stimulating and challenging. Having designed many art gallery roofs since Menil, Renzo's challenge to me at the start of a recent new project was 'building on our 35 years' shared experience, what can we do differently and better this time?' This sums up Renzo's constant science-based experimentation, which underpins his architecture.

A Scientific Architect
Eric Kandel

The interior of the
Jerome L. Greene
Science Center at
Columbia University's
Manhattanville
Campus, New York

When Lee Bollinger became Columbia University's President in 2002, he
was struck by the fact that the university was space-poor. There was simply
nowhere to add new buildings on the existing campus. Other universities
facing a similar problem had scattered buildings across their respective
cities, but in Columbia's case there was an alternative solution. Just north
of the existing campus, and almost as large again, was an area called
Manhattanville (pp. 80–81), at that time largely empty. It was on this site
that I first met Renzo Piano, the architect responsible for Columbia's
Manhattanville project and – throughout the process - a true collaborator.

In December 2017 I had the opportunity to visit Renzo's office in Paris
and I was immensely impressed by the rigour and attention accorded to
everything – from the smallest detail to the larger creative picture. His
architecture practice appeared to me to be an extraordinary scientific
enterprise. The scientific approach was seen both in the ordering systems
he uses for his ideas and projects, and in his enthusiasm for his work.
I understood that the members of the Building Workshop were not just
interested in designing façades but were deeply involved with the practical
and functional aspects of a building – its constructability, efficiency and
sustainability. They were interested in the details, discussing with my fellow
neuroscientists things like spatial organisation, ergonomics, materials,
colours and finishes which they reviewed together in mock-ups. Our
discussions ranged even wider – from how birds communicate to how
the human brain responds to taste, colour and light... I felt that Renzo truly
understood that in expanding the university's campus, we were pursuing
the expansion of the university's academic mission.

In order better to understand its environment and working methods,
Antoine Chaaya, the lead architect on the project, and his team from the
Paris office, visited the laboratory at Columbia where they participated in
a Polymerase Chain Reaction experiment, a laboratory technique allowing
multiple copies of a segment of DNA to be made. I spoke with Antoine

A plan of the second
floor of the Jerome L.
Greene Science Center

about what neuroscience can tell us about art and architecture and discovered that we had a similar approach to research: 'watching in the dark', meaning simply that a scientist or architect must keep his or her eyes open without having made premeditated decisions. In other words, research and creativity work in the same way – one must work without an ulterior motive to avoid repeating what one has done before. During this visit, we found a common ground in the relationship between art and science, and between architecture and science.

Morningside Heights, the original campus of Columbia University, was built in the late nineteenth century by McKim, Mead & White, then one of the leading architectural firms in America. Their classical-style buildings, quiet quadrangles and impressive gates set the campus and its students apart from the outside world. Although this was not necessarily a negative thing, Renzo could immediately see when Bollinger approached him that, in comparison, the new campus could be radically different, a freer space, open to its surroundings and the community.

In creating an expanded home for Columbia, Renzo aimed to 'reflect a shift in society' – a similar aim, he has said, to that with which he approached the Centre Pompidou (pp. 36–39).[1] In this case, we were coming to a shared vision of what a twenty-first-century campus should look like, and how it should relate to its host city. We wanted the university, its research, its faculty and its students to be accessible to the vibrancy of the surrounding West Harlem area, and vice versa. Pedestrian paths would 'invite residents into the academic sphere'.[2] The first two buildings that Bollinger asked Piano to design were the Jerome L. Greene Science Center and the Lenfest Center for the Arts, both completed in 2016. Public access to the ground floor of both buildings with shops, an exhibition space and cafés allows a flow of people through the space, and fosters interaction between members of the public, students and academic staff.

Of the Greene Center, Piano has said, 'It is a palace of light. Its transparency is meant to underscore that the knowledge being generated inside is for the public and will be shared with them.'[3] Within the building, the feeling of transparency remains. The brain is very sensitive to light, as well as colours, movement, hearing, vision and surroundings. The building offers a space to experience these naturally on a daily basis. Offices and lab spaces are located at the perimeter, so as to take advantage of natural light, with support spaces, which do not require daylight, at the core of the building.

My new office at the Greene Center is in the corner of the building – one of four corner spaces usually used as interactive and informal meeting rooms. The new office has had a transformative effect on my working patterns; it is quite different from my office at Washington Heights. Other people can see what I am doing and I can see what they are doing. The building is planned to encourage circulation and interaction, interspersing formal seminar rooms and common break-out spaces with research and offices over double height spaces, so we meet colleagues by just walking down the hall or up or down a flight of stairs. It generates a much more social environment, which encourages creative interaction and brings greater ease of access to my colleagues.

When speaking to Renzo, I most enjoyed his curiosity about how the individual responds to his architecture – how they might *enjoy* living and working in the space he has created. Brancusi said something similar: 'What really matters in art is joy. You don't need to understand. Does what you contemplate make you happy? That is the only thing that counts.'

When a new building is finished, Renzo likes to go incognito, staying and watching people move around the space he has created. He says that he knows he's done his job if people look happy. From a neuroscientist's perspective, I know that the brain's major response to beauty is joy, and it is with an enormous sense of pleasure that I respond to the spaces. He has created a true forum for the exchange of ideas and energy within the university and between the university and its surrounding community. His architecture itself encourages creativity and interaction, and it is likely to bring out the very best in all of us.

Human Colour
Luis Fernández-Galiano

The architecture of Renzo Piano is more humanist than technological. If there is something that threads together his works, it is attention to people, who from escalators at the Centre Pompidou (pp. 36–39) are treated to the spectacle of the Parisian square or who from a raised platform at the Centro Botín (pp. 88–91) can contemplate the serene and shifting beauty of the Bay of Santander. Although in many cases there are elements of factory aesthetics, the outward expression of the construction is not as important as the experience of those moving inside – or outside – the building. And the pleasure of moving up and down stairs in search of objectives or views is complemented by the pleasure of seeing people in motion, introducing the warmth of life into the exact geometries of construction. A case in point is the Whitney Museum (pp. 82–83), whose exterior stairs are always being used, even in drizzle or cold. So is the headquarters of The New York Times (pp. 64–67), which puts its interior stairs along the façade to make ascending and descending them more pleasurable, and to make the skyscraper less an impenetrable monolith than a building that opens to the street by showing the lively hustle and bustle inside.

Although it is inevitable to emphasise the importance of construction or the supreme elegance of the design of the pieces, the technical sophistication of Piano's work is put at the service of people, thus complying with a now almost extinct tradition: the moral commitment of modernity. The Genoese architect spent a critical stage of his training in London and it was there – in the restless crucible of the Architectural Association – that he met Richard Rogers, who had recently terminated his association with Norman Foster in the framework of Team 4 and with whom Piano was to embark on the adventure of the competition for the Centre Pompidou. Their long-lasting friendship, which extended beyond the period of their partnership, was strengthened by their Mediterranean characters and roots, but also by their joint belief in the moral commitment of architecture, always more significant than their technological interests. A year after the opening of Beaubourg, the label 'high-tech' was coined, a term which in the field of architecture would be associated essentially with three names, Foster, Rogers, and Piano, from then on tied to innovation and technology (though sadly their shared interest in the ethical dimension of the discipline, which postmodernity had considered all but finished, was pushed to the background).

Reyner Banham was the critic most sympathetic towards this technical approach. At his death in 1988 he left an incomplete and unpublished book about high-tech, salvaged by Todd Gannon from the historian's archives at the Getty Research Institute.[1] Banham summarised high-tech in three features: exposed services, exposed structure and bold colours. This, while a good description of the Centre Pompidou, definitely does not apply to the later works of the architects (although Foster's HSBC Building in Hong Kong, Rogers's Lloyd's Building in London and Piano's Kansai International Airport [pp. 48–49] are still close to this canonical definition). Banham admired the way that Alfred Barr, in his foreword to *The International Style*, the catalogue of the 1932 exhibition curated by Henry-Russell Hitchcock and Philip Johnson at the Museum of Modern Art in New York, synthesised the aesthetic principles of the style - volumes delimited by planes that evoke neither mass nor solidness; regularity instead of symmetry; and elegance of materials, techniques and proportions as opposed to applied ornament - and coined his own triad for the high-tech style, with the three characteristics mentioned above.[2] Nonetheless, greater familiarity with the work of Piano - the IBM Travelling Pavilion (pp. 44–45), about which he published sharp analyses; the Menil Collection (pp. 40–43), whose light he described as 'honest, pellucid and without additives'; or the Lowara office building, with its suspended roof facilitating environmental control - together with Foster's growing distance from conventional high technology led Banham to modify that motto in his latest writings, establishing in its place the three features of 'ethical modernism': clarity, honesty and unity, where architectural ethics is understood as the combination of constructional excellence and social responsibility.

These features, which essentially refer to the timeless principles of architecture, describe Piano's work well, as much the early works that Banham got to know as the more recent ones: clarity in structural articulation, honesty in service to function and aesthetic unity between the parts and the whole. Piano's buildings are assembled piece by piece, but the pieces come together clearly, are subordinated to criteria of use and belong to a coherent entity. These characteristics define an aesthetic with classicist roots, but also an aesthetic of modern inspiration because the limelight is always on people. Whether in busy contexts like those mentioned above - the Centre Pompidou, the Whitney Museum and the Centro Botín - or in spaces conceived for contemplation - the Menil

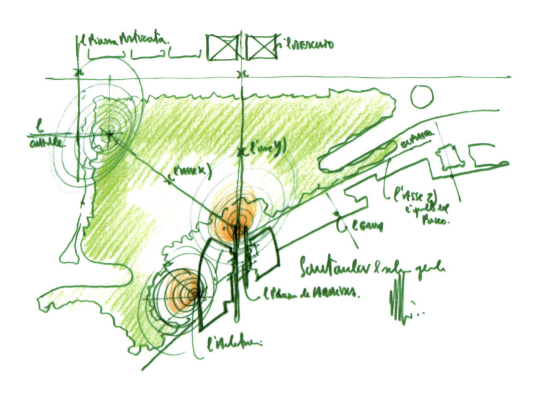

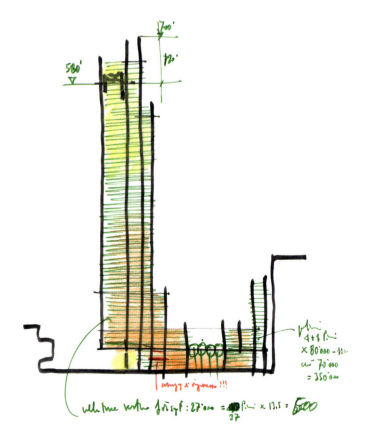

Collection, the Beyeler Foundation or the Nasher Sculpture Center, for example – and whether the venues are hectic or placid, in all cases the interpretation of the place and the client's demands – so often inseparable from the building, be they those of Georges and Claude Pompidou, Emilio Botín, Dominique de Menil, Ernst Beyeler or Raymond Nasher – are expressed in terms of the visitor's experience. Through his work, Piano has always pursued the reconciliation of technical innovation and social duty, guided by what he calls 'the inner compass' built inside him during childhood and early youth, and which still today orients his defence of the civic dimension and social function of architecture, be it in the building commissions or in his generous pro-bono dedication to the improvement of urban peripheries with a team of young architects whom he pays out of his stipend as Italian Life Senator.

Renzo Piano always draws with a green felt-tip pen and has made that green an almost heraldic colour, using it in his stationery and in the logo of the foundation that bears his name. In his plans, however, the dominant colour is a bright orange that saturates the more public zones of his buildings, the most intensely used spaces, or those most circulated in. The warm tones, which allude to human presence, are not really thermographs but statements of intention, making it visible in the project that the building is there to serve people, as the purpose of a construction is to be inhabited. This human warmth is what justifies the description of Piano's architecture as 'more humanist than technological', because the elegance of details and masterly manipulation of natural light are nothing without the perception – whether attentive or distracted – of the visitor, who is, in the end, the true protagonist of the building and of architecture itself. From the green of nature and sustainability to the bright orange of human warmth, Piano's commitment to the public realm is the true legacy of his architecture and of his life.

Why I Love the Architect Renzo Piano
Roberto Benigni

Renzo Piano and Roberto Benigni sailing in June 2010

Allegro con brio

Because he's Italian

Because the Italians invented architecture and Renzo Piano is the most Italian of architects

Because he has the rhythm of Horace, the majesty of Virgil, the festive charm of Ovid

Because he's Genoese

Because he's Genoese and generous

Because once he invited me to his workshop in Genoa. I thought I'd got the wrong address. From ground level, I couldn't see anything. Then, from nowhere, an elevator appeared, like the train on Platform 9¾ in Harry Potter. I went up with him through a narrow gorge and at the end of the journey everything broadened out and became limitless. Wrapped in sea air and water from the sky, a form appeared in the light, ready for take off. Inside, a hundred apprentices moved about in a whirlwind of gestures and tools. He asked me if I'd like to have lunch with him there. I said yes. It was the first time I'd had lunch on a butterfly's wings

Because Renzo Piano is master of the art that transforms deserts into gardens and builds up marvels to the sky

Because he's a senator for life, but does not live like a senator

Because he doesn't know love for power, but knows the power of love

Because the restoration of the Lingotto in Turin is a masterpiece

Because Baudelaire said: '*...tu m'as donné ta boue et j'en ai fait de l'or.*' You gave me your mud and I made some gold

Because he loves having fun and when he tells a joke he never remembers the punchline and it makes you die laughing

Because when he's with friends, always, at the end of every lunch or dinner, he pulls out a coloured marker pen and begins to talk and draw scribbles and figures on the napkins, plates, tablecloth. The restaurant owners smile happily because they think the drawings will be theirs. But not when I'm there. When I'm there I take it all. Including the plates and the tablecloth

Because Renzo Piano makes architecture out of anything

Because he builds for human beings, not for his own brand

Because the stadium in Bari is a masterpiece, even more beautiful than the Millennium Falcon

Because in some of his buildings even the smallest stone is imbued with the infinite

Because at a certain point he pulls a tape measure out of his pocket and begins measuring everything that comes to hand. Objects and people

Because his buildings are the 'masterly, correct and magnificent interplay of masses brought together in light'. They incorporate solidity, utility and grace. *Firmitas, utilitas, venustas*

Because one evening in Paris in the rain we got talking about Brunelleschi and he pulled out a coloured marker pen and his tape measure and calculated and drew the plan of Santa Maria del Fiore on the flagstones of a *palazzo* in Rue des Archives with such creative self-confidence that that evening I was not talking *about* Brunelleschi, I was talking *to* Brunelleschi

Because Renzo Piano, like Brunelleschi, doesn't build just to accommodate a community but to move it

Because the Nemo Centre in Amsterdam is a ship that can fly

Because the Tjibaou Centre in New Caledonia is a radiant marvel. And it reminds us that art can never be modern, it always goes back to its origins

Because he never makes us feel where nature ends and art begins

Because not long ago Nicoletta and I went to the Whitney Museum to see Hopper, de Kooning, Warhol, and when we came back we were talking about light, form, colour, perspective, innovation, simplicity, lines, complexity, beauty; but we weren't talking about the paintings, we were talking about the museum

Because he loves music

Because Vitruvius said that architecture is the sister of music

Because the Auditorium in Rome is a masterpiece. Look for yourself and you'll find the accent, the opening notes, *legato, staccato, vibrato, rallentando, accelerando*. A concerto

Because Leon Battista Alberti wrote in *De re aedificatoria*: 'Beauty is a concerto of all the parts fitted together in proportion and connection.'

Because I met Renzo Piano at the Auditorium in Rome at a concert with Claudio Abbado. It was a great spectacle. Yes!

Because Renzo Piano and Claudio Abbado together were a great spectacle

Because I have been with them many times and have watched them carefully, to understand the way a friendship is built, elusive and tender

Because in an interview about the Centre Pompidou, Renzo Piano said that a museum shouldn't feel sacred or intimidating. But when I saw Beaubourg for the first time in '79, I stood silently like the Greeks in front of their sacred objects and I was intimidated. Yes, I was scared

Because all novelty frightens, even happiness

Because Beaubourg is a wonderful object, an astounding undertaking which leaves you speechless

Because it is impossible to tie down ecstasy with analysis

Because he loves literature and film. He knows about geometry, factories, distances, movement and the very appearance of the universe. With his buildings he lends us wings so we can travel the heavens

Because the Shard in London is terrifying. With a single act of violence it twists man in the direction of angels

Because the first time I saw it, at dawn one day in October, I thought of Shakespeare's words in Sonnet 29: 'Like to the lark at break of day arising / From sullen earth sings hymns at heaven's gate'

Because one day he introduced me to Richard Rogers. I watched them together for a whole long afternoon and finally came to understand how the palace of friendship is built

Because Renzo Piano is an honest and faithful friend. Content and curious. Fragile and indestructible. Crystal and steel

Because he has a marvellous woman by his side

Because he has made his life into a masterpiece

Because he's not a star architect

Because he is an architect

Because he is a star

Endnotes

An Architect of Dignity
Kate Goodwin (pp. 11–19)

1. C. P. Cavafy, 'The City', from *C. P. Cavafy: Collected Poems*, translated by Edmund Keeley and Philip Sherrard, Princeton, 1975.
2. Renzo Piano and Kenneth Frampton, *Renzo Piano: The Complete Logbook*, London, 2016.
3. The author in conversation with Renzo Piano, September 2016.
4. Lorenzo Ciccarelli, *Renzo Piano Before Renzo Piano: Masters and Beginnings*, Macerata, 2017, p. 56.
5. After seeing his early structural experiments at the Architectural Association in London, Pidgeon, writing in an issue of *AD* (March 1970), put Renzo in a category of 'architects … [such as Mies van der Rohe and Nervi] who found complete absorption in the manipulation and developments of pure structural systems in relation to human requirements for shelter, comfort and functionally useable space'.
6. Peter Buchanan, *Renzo Piano Building Workshop, Complete Work, Volume One*, London, 1993, p. 30.
7. Renzo Piano interviewed for the e^2 podcast episode 'The Art and Science of Renzo Piano', January 2009.
8. Charles Dickens, *Pictures from Italy*, New York, 1874, p. 37.
9. 'Facciamo cose che Fanno città: Un'intervista a Renzo Piano', *Abitare*, 28 August 2009.
10. C. P. Cavafy, 'The City'.

In Bottega
Fulvio Irace (pp. 103–09)

1. Fulvio Irace, 'Renzo Piano festeggia gli 80 anni in "bottega"', *Il Sole 24*, 14 September 2017.
2. Quoted in Fulvio Irace (ed.), *Renzo Piano: Visible Cities*, Milan, 2007, p. 11.
3. Ibid.
4. Renzo Piano, 'Pezzo per pezzo', in Gianpiero Donini (ed.), *Renzo Piano. Pezzo per pezzo*, Rome, 1982.
5. Quoted in Irace, *Visible Cities*, p. 11.
6. Reyner Banham, *The Architecture of the Well-tempered Environment*, London, 1969, p. 255.
7. Piano was not indifferent to either group; some of their work appears on the photographic panels in the exhibition 'Mutazioni della forma in architettura', curated by him for the XIV Triennale in Milan in 1968. See Paola Nicolin, *Castelli di carte. La XIV Triennale di Milano*, Macerata and Rome, 2011.
8. Sonja Hildebrand and Elisabeth Bergmann (eds), *Form-finding, Form-shaping, Designing Architecture: Experimental, Aesthetic and Ethical Approaches to Form in Architecture from the Postwar Period to Today*, Mendrisio, 2016.
9. Quoted in Irace, *Visible Cities*, p. 10.
10. Ibid., pp. 11–12.
11. Ibid., p. 11.
12. Lorenzo Ciccarelli, 'Philadelphia Connections in Renzo Piano's Formative Years: Robert Le

Ricolais and Louis I. Kahn', *Construction History*, 31, 2, 2016, pp. 201–22.
13. Lorenzo Ciccarelli, *Renzo Piano prima di Renzo Piano*, Macerata, 2017, pp. 249–61.

London, Fifty Years Ago
Lorenzo Ciccarelli (pp. 111–15)

1. Lorenzo Ciccarelli, *Renzo Piano before Renzo Piano: Masters and Beginnings*, Macerata, 2017, pp. 185–88.
2. Ibid., pp. 265–78.
3. As an example, see Massimo Teodori, *Architettura e città in Gran Bretagna*, Bologna, 1967.
4. Elain Harwood, *Space, Hope and Brutalism: English Architecture 1945–75*, New Haven and London, 2015. See in particular pp. 84–88 and 169–85.
5. Renzo Piano was responsible for a buildings laboratory in which students built small structures and pavilions in the gardens of Bedford Square; see Enrique Walker, 'In Conversation with Renzo Piano and Richard Rogers', *AA Files*, 70, 2015, pp. 46–59.
6. The early career of the British architect is described in the first chapters of Richard Rogers, *A Place for All People: Life, Architecture and the Fair Society*, Edinburgh, 2017.
7. See Renzo Piano, 'Architecture and Technology', *Architectural Design*, 6–7, 1970, pp. 140–45.
8. See Susan Holden, 'Possible Pompidous', *AA Files*, 70, 2015, pp. 33–45 for a review of the proposals submitted to the competition for the Centre Pompidou. On the events leading up to the design of the outside space and the building of Beaubourg, see Francesco Dal Co, *Centre Pompidou: Renzo Piano, Richard Rogers and the Making of a Modern Monument*, New Haven and London, 2016. See also Renzo Piano and Richard *Rogers, Piano + Rogers: Centre Pompidou*, Genoa, 2017.

Being a Client
Paul Winkler (pp. 123–31)

1. *The Menil Collection: A Selection from the Paleolithic to the Modern Era*, New York, 1987.
2. Reyner Banham, 'In the Neighbourhood of Art', *Art in America*, June 1987, pp. 124–29

A Scientific Architect
Eric Kandel (pp. 141–43)

1. Renzo Piano, 'Manhattanville: Columbia's bold vision for a new city campus begins to take shape.', *Columbia Magazine*, Spring 2017.
2. Ibid.
3. Ibid.

Human Colour
Luis Fernández-Galiano (pp. 145–49)

1. See Todd Gannon, *Reyner Banham and the Paradoxes of High Tech*, Los Angeles, 2017.
2. See Henry Russell Hitchcock and Philip Johnson, *The International Style*, exh. cat., Museum of Modern Art, 1932.

Further Reading

Reyner Banham, *The Architecture of the Well-tempered Environment*, London, 1969

'Being Renzo Piano', *Abitare*, 497, November 2009

Peter Buchanan, *Renzo Piano Building Workshop: Complete Works*, vols 1-5, London and New York, 1993-2008

Lorenzo Ciccarelli, *Renzo Piano Before Renzo Piano: Masters and Beginnings*, Macerata, 2017

Francesco Dal Co, *Centre Pompidou: Renzo Piano, Richard Rogers and the Making of a Modern Monument*, New Haven and London, 2016

Philip Jodidio, *Piano*, Cologne, 2012

Philip Jodidio, *Piano: Renzo Piano Building Workshop 1966 to Today*, Cologne, 2008

Aymeric Lorente, *Architecture and Music: Renzo Piano Building Workshop – Seven Sites for Music*, Milan, 2002

Victoria Newhouse, *Renzo Piano Museums*, New York, 2007

Renzo Piano, *On Tour with Renzo Piano*, London and New York, 2004

Renzo Piano and Kenneth Frampton, *Renzo Piano: The Complete Logbook*, London, 2016

Renzo Piano, 'Architecture and Technology', *Architectural Design*, 6-7, 1970, pp. 140-45

'Renzo Piano Building Workshop 2007-17', *AV Monographs*, 197-98, 2017

Peter Rice, *An Engineer Imagines*, London, 1994

Richard Rogers, *A Place for All People: Life, Architecture and the Fair Society*, Edinburgh, 2017

The following publications on specific projects, listed by publication date, are published by the Fondazione Renzo Piano.

Nouméa: Centre Culturel Jean-Marie Tjibaou, 2008

Beyeler: Fondation Beyeler, 2011

Menil: The Menil Collection, 2011

San Francisco: California Academy of Sciences, 2011

The Shard: London Bridge Quarter, 2012

Ronchamp: Ronchamp Monastery, 2014

Whitney: Whitney Museum of American Art, 2015

Athens: Stavros Niarchos Foundation Cultural Center, 2016

Centre Pompidou, 2018

Image Credits

Every attempt has been made to trace the copyright holders of works reproduced. Specific acknowledgements are as follows:

Richard Bradley / Alamy Stock Photo: page 114

Photo © Michel Denancé: pages 38 (beneath), 46, 60, 63, 64–67, 70, 71, 76, 77–79, 98, 102, 110, 136, 144; page 53 (ADCK - Centre Culturel Tjibaou)

© Richard Einzig / arcaidimages.com: page 147

© Gianni Berengo Gardin: pages 10, 14–17, 39, 44, 45, 47

Photo © Tim Griffith: page 6

Photo © Paul Hester. Courtesy of The Menil Collection, Houston: pages 40–41

Photo: Lehnartz/ullstein bild via Getty Images: page 107

© Charles Leonard / Shutterstock: pages 36–37

© Chris Martin / www.chrismartinphotographer. com: pages 72–73

Courtesy of RPBW / Fondazione Renzo Piano: cover sketches, pages 13, 34, 35 (above and beneath), 104, 109, 112, 115, 124, 126, 127, 128, 137, 140, 142, 148 (above and beneath), 150; cover portrait, page 157 (above and beneath) (Photo: Stefano Goldberg); page 2 (Photo: Fregoso & Basalto); page 4 (Photo: Studio Fotografico Merlo); pages 19, 20, 22–31, 49, 68, 69, 101, 125, 134, 135 (Photo: Shunji Ishida); page 38 (above) (Photo: Francesca Avanzinelli); pages 42, 131 (Hickey & Robertson Photography); page 43 (Photo: Paul Hester); pages 50–52 (Photo: Sergio Grazia / ADCK - Centre Culturel Tjibaou); pages 54–55 (Photo: Vincent Mosch); pages 56, 88–90 (Photo: Enrico Cano); pages 57–59 (Photo: Moreno Maggi); page 62 (Photo: Serge Drouin); page 74 (Photo: Andrew Meredith); page 75 (Photo: Nikolas Ventourakis); pages 80–81 (Courtesy Columbia University. Photo: Nic Lehoux); pages 82, 83 (Photo: Nic Lehoux); pages 84–85 (© SNFCC. Photo: Yiorgis Yerolymbos); pages 86–87 (© National Library of Greece / Nikos Karanikolas); pages 92–93 (Photo: Sergio Grazia); page 94 (© A.M.P.A.S.); page 95 (© Archivio Emergency); page 100 (Photo: Jacques Minassian); page 116 (© Susumu Shingu); page 118 (© Yasuko Shingu / Susumu Shingu); page 119 (Photo: Shunji Ishida. © Susumu Shingu); page 121 (© SNFCC. Photo: George Dimitrakopoulous); page 122 (Robertson Photography); page 132 (Photo: Justin Lee); page 138 (© ARUP)

Cedric Price fonds / Canadian Centre for Architecture: page 113

© Paul Raftery: pages 8–9

© 2018. Photo Scala, Florence: page 106

© Viewpictures. Photo: Dennis Gilbert: page 48

The Renzo Piano Building Workshop
at Punta Nave, Genoa, 2016

The Renzo Piano Building Workshop
at Rue des Archives, Paris, 2016

Index

First published on the occasion of the exhibition 'Renzo Piano: The Art of Making Buildings'

Royal Academy of Arts, London, 15 September 2018 – 20 January 2019

Exhibition organised by the Royal Academy of Arts, London, in collaboration with Renzo Piano Building Workshop and the Fondazione Renzo Piano

With thanks to
Renzo Piano
Giorgio Bianchi
Shunji Ishida
Milly Rossato-Piano
with
Chiara Bennati
Stefania Canta
Chiara Casazza
Lorenzo Ciccarelli
Nicoletta Durante
Giulia Giglio
Andrea Malgeri
Elena Spadavecchia
and
Mehdi Cupaiolo
Philippe Goubet
Antonio Porcile
Giuseppe Semprini
Nicola Serpico

Exhibition Curators
Kate Goodwin
assisted by
Lucy Chiswell

Artistic Director
Tim Marlow

Exhibition Management
Stephanie Bush
assisted by
Nancy Cooper

Photographic and Copyright Coordination
Giulia Ariete

Lenders to the Exhibition
Renzo Piano Building Workshop
Fondazione Renzo Piano
Daimler Art Collection, Stuttgart/Berlin
Tony Fretton
Gianni Berengo Gardin
Rogers Stirk Harbour + Partners

Royal Academy Publications
Florence Dassonville, *Production Coordinator*
Rosie Hore, *Project Editor*
Carola Krueger, *Production Manager*
Peter Sawbridge, *Editorial Director*
Nick Tite, *Publisher*

Translation from the Italian (Fulvio Irace and Roberto Benigni): Caroline Beamish

Translation from the Japanese (Susumu Shingu): Ann B. Cary

Design: Jon Kielty
Typeset in Forma DJR
Indexing: Hilary Bird
Colour origination: DawkinsColour
Printed in Italy by Printer Trento

British Library Cataloguing-in-Publication Data

A catalogue record for this book is available from the British Library

ISBN 978-1910350713

Distributed outside the United States and Canada by ACC Art Books, Suffolk, Woodbridge, IP12 4SD

Distributed in the United States and Canada by ARTBOOK | D.A.P., 2nd Floor, 155 6th Avenue, New York, NY 10013

Illustrations
Page 2: the model-making workshop at Punta Nave

Page 4: Punta Nave

Pages 8–9: the Jérôme Seydoux Pathé Foundation, Paris

Supported by

ROCCO FORTE HOTELS

Supported by

www.turkishceramics.com

Lighting Partner

Supported by

ITALIAN TRADE AGENCY
ICE - Italian Trade Commission
Trade Promotion Section of the Italian Embassy

Supported by

Scott and Laura Malkin